DC COMICS

The UNTOLD
LEGEND
of the
BAT MAN ™

Written by
LEN WEIN

Illustrated by
JIM APARO · JOHN BYRNE

TOR

A TOM DOHERTY ASSOCIATES BOOK
NEW YORK

THE UNTOLD LEGEND OF THE BATMAN

A Tom Doherty Associates original.

Edited by Andrew Helfer.

Interior design and production by Bob Rozakis, Jodi Saviuk and
Alex Saviuk.

ISBN: 0-812-50353-8   Can. ISBN: 0-812-50352-X

Printed in the United States of America

First Printing: August. 1982

10   9   8

INTRODUCTION TO AN INTRODUCTION

In 1939 *Detective Comics* featured a story called "The Case of the Chemical Syndicate". The seemingly innocuous tale opened with a scene of Commissioner Gordon of Gotham City chatting with his friend, socialite Bruce Wayne. Later in the story a mysterious cloaked figure appeared who not only solved the case Gordon was working on, but also single-handedly brought the criminals to justice. He was called The Bat-Man. Little more was said to explain The Bat-Man's mysterious crusade against the criminal element of the world. His motives remained his own. The only other insight we received into his personality was his secret indentity. In the last panel of the story it was revealed that Bruce Wayne was The Bat-Man!

That was it. It wasn't much of a beginning. His predecessor, and soon to be close friend, Superman, had an entire page to tell of his beginnings, but The Bat-Man had to wait six more issues of *Detective Comics* before he was looked upon with enough regard to be given a history, and then only two pages worth. For almost nine years the stalker of human vermin remained as much an enigma to his faithful readers as he was to his notorious prey until editor Mort Weisinger commissioned writer Bill Finger to draft a full history of the cowled sleuth. It appeared as a single story in 1948, in *Batman* #47. By now The Batman had dropped the hyphen.

Had The Batman followed most of his costumed contemporaries to oblivion, that one story would probably have been enough. But The Batman proved that he was even tougher than the super-powered crime-busters of his time. Because of his vulnerability, he had only his wit and courage to shield him against the ruthless attacks from the soldiers of crime. Cut him and he would bleed. Shove the muzzle of a tommy-gun into his ribs and he was scared. It was, perhaps, this humanity which allowed The Batman not only to endure but also to flourish. His family of crime-fighters grew and he added some of the most infamous and, at the same time, the most unforgettable villains to his Rogues Gallery.

The time has come for a more lengthy retelling of The Batman Legend. But for those of you who expect to find no more than a rehashing of oft-told tales, you are in for a most surprising and pleasurable experience. Writer Len Wein has woven together the human histories of The Batman and his friends and foes into a brilliant psychological thriller which will keep you hooked right up to its shattering climax, when The Batman confronts his most deadly antagonist.

In page after well-crafted page, artists Jim Aparo and John Byrne follow the Darknight Detective through the back alleys and smokey after-hour hangouts of Gotham City's Underworld Figures. The tension of every panel is heightened by the drama of their fine layouts and foreboding shadows.

Besides the tribulations or our brooding hero, you will learn several little-known facts which Wein has cleverly peppered into this exciting yarn. Who, for example, were the first people to wear a Batman and Robin costume? The obvious answers are not necessarily the correct ones.

If you are looking for a book of facts about one of the most fascinating characters in fiction, this book is for you. If, instead, you have a hankering for a fast-paced thriller then…this is ALSO for you.

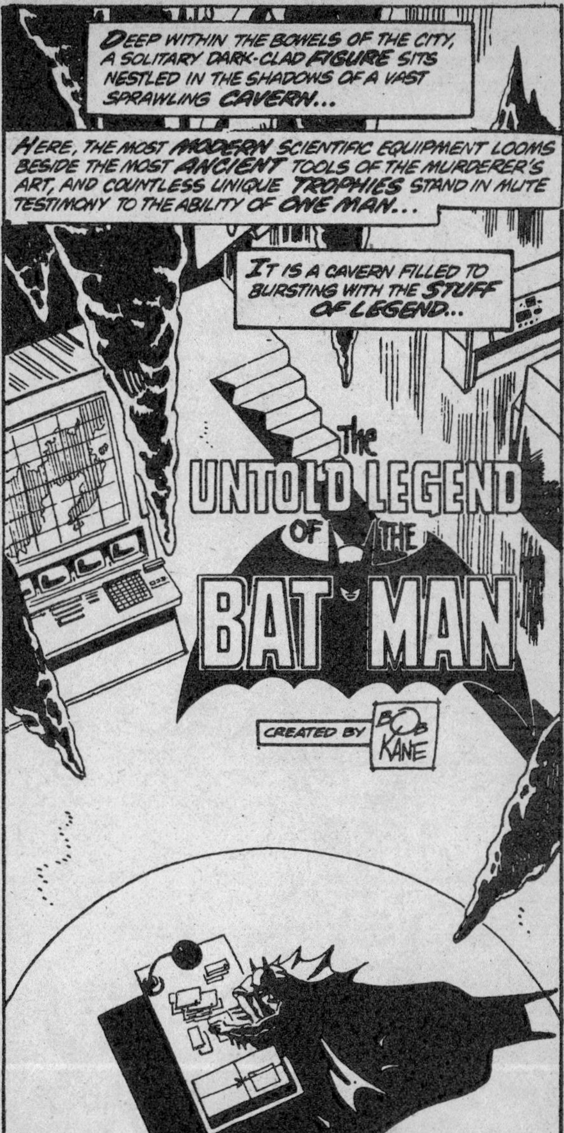
DEEP WITHIN THE BOWELS OF THE CITY, A SOLITARY DARK-CLAD FIGURE SITS NESTLED IN THE SHADOWS OF A VAST SPRAWLING CAVERN...
HERE, THE MOST MODERN SCIENTIFIC EQUIPMENT LOOMS BESIDE THE MOST ANCIENT TOOLS OF THE MURDERER'S ART, AND COUNTLESS UNIQUE TROPHIES STAND IN MUTE TESTIMONY TO THE ABILITY OF ONE MAN...
IT IS A CAVERN FILLED TO BURSTING WITH THE STUFF OF LEGEND...
THE UNTOLD LEGEND OF THE BATMAN
CREATED BY BOB KANE

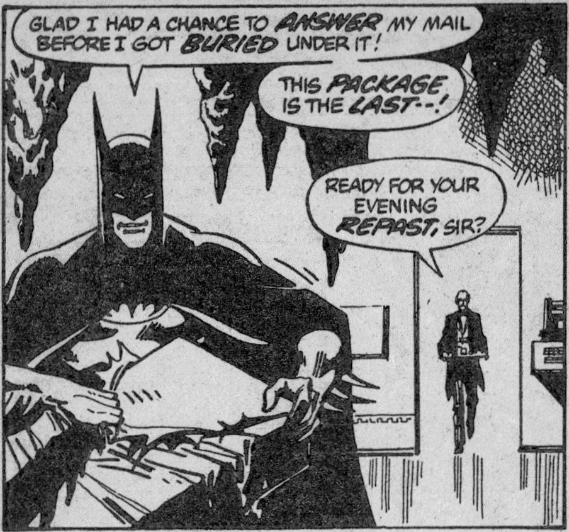
GLAD I HAD A CHANCE TO ANSWER MY MAIL BEFORE I GOT BURIED UNDER IT!
THIS PACKAGE IS THE LAST--!
READY FOR YOUR EVENING REPAST, SIR?

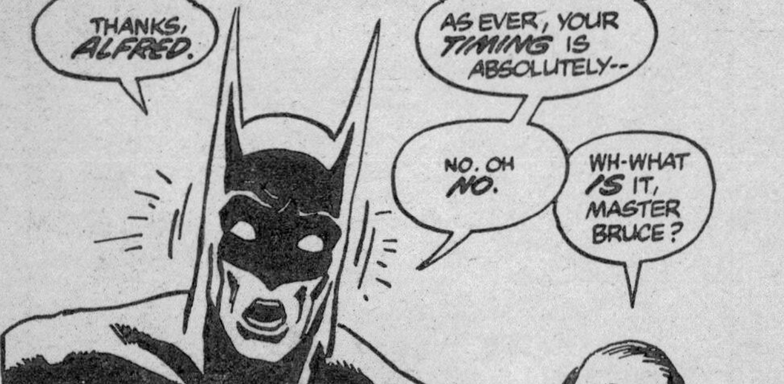
THANKS, ALFRED.
AS EVER, YOUR TIMING IS ABSOLUTELY--
NO. OH NO.
WH-WHAT IS IT, MASTER BRUCE?

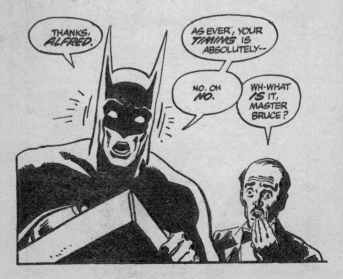

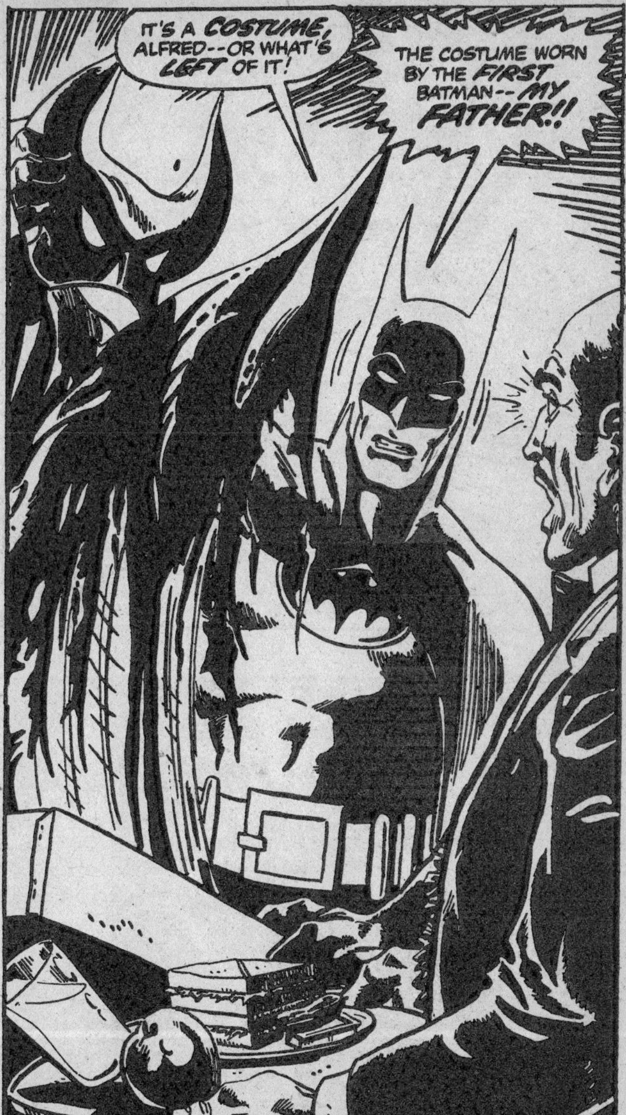
IT'S A COSTUME, ALFRED--OR WHAT'S LEFT OF IT!
THE COSTUME WORN BY THE FIRST BATMAN--MY FATHER!!

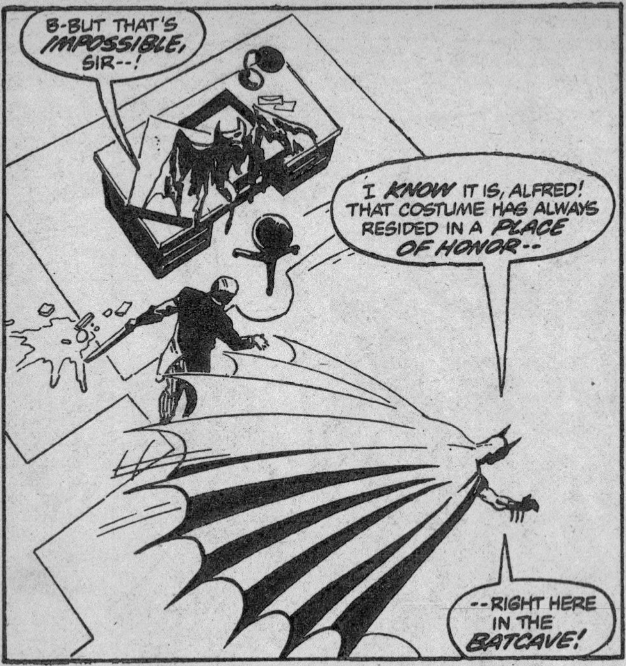
B-BUT THAT'S IMPOSSIBLE, SIR--!
I KNOW IT IS, ALFRED! THAT COSTUME HAS ALWAYS RESIDED IN A PLACE OF HONOR--
--RIGHT HERE IN THE BATCAVE!

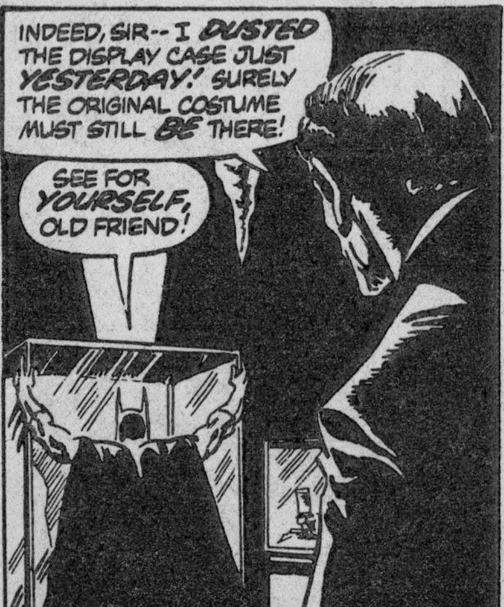
INDEED, SIR-- I DUSTED THE DISPLAY CASE JUST YESTERDAY! SURELY THE ORIGINAL COSTUME MUST STILL BE THERE!
SEE FOR YOURSELF, OLD FRIEND!

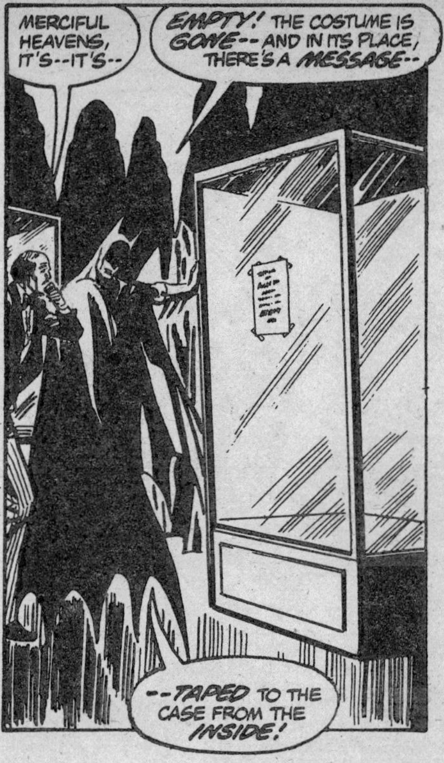
MERCIFUL HEAVENS, IT'S--IT'S--
EMPTY! THE COSTUME IS GONE--AND IN ITS PLACE, THERE'S A MESSAGE--
--TAPED TO THE CASE FROM THE INSIDE!

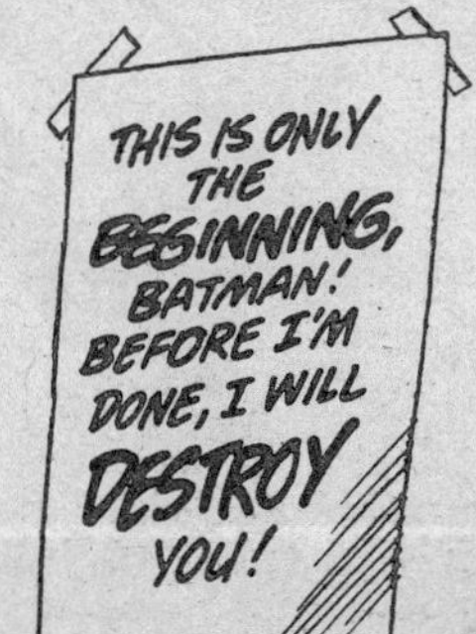
THIS IS ONLY THE BEGINNING, BATMAN! BEFORE I'M DONE, I WILL DESTROY YOU!

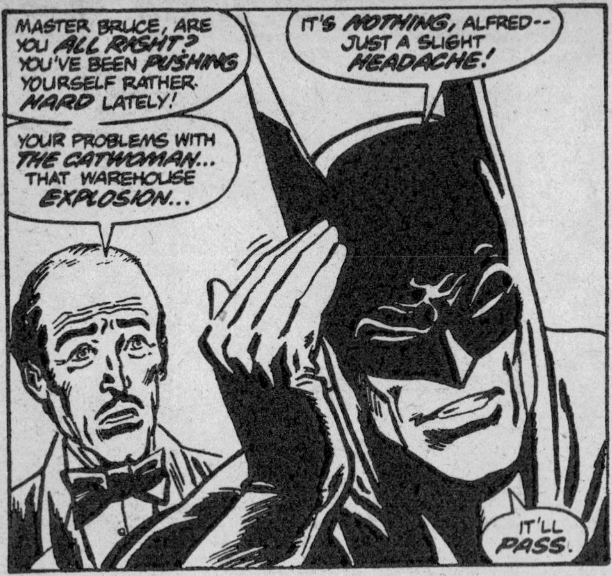
MASTER BRUCE, ARE YOU ALL RIGHT? YOU'VE BEEN PUSHING YOURSELF RATHER HARD LATELY!
YOUR PROBLEMS WITH THE CATWOMAN... THAT WAREHOUSE EXPLOSION...
IT'S NOTHING, ALFRED-- JUST A SLIGHT HEADACHE!
IT'LL PASS.

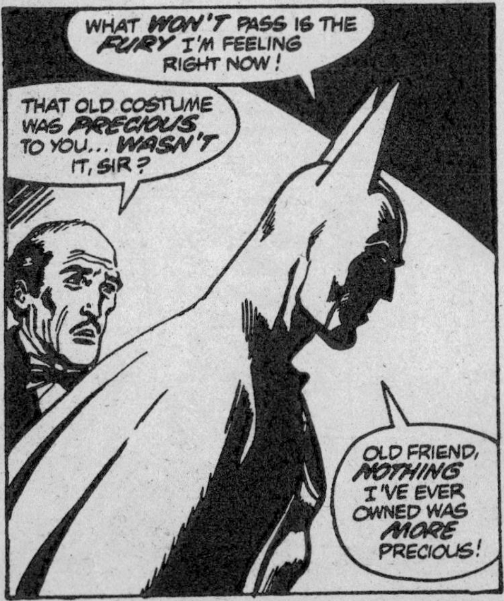
WHAT WON'T PASS IS THE FURY I'M FEELING RIGHT NOW!
THAT OLD COSTUME WAS PRECIOUS TO YOU... WASN'T IT, SIR?
OLD FRIEND, NOTHING I'VE EVER OWNED WAS MORE PRECIOUS!

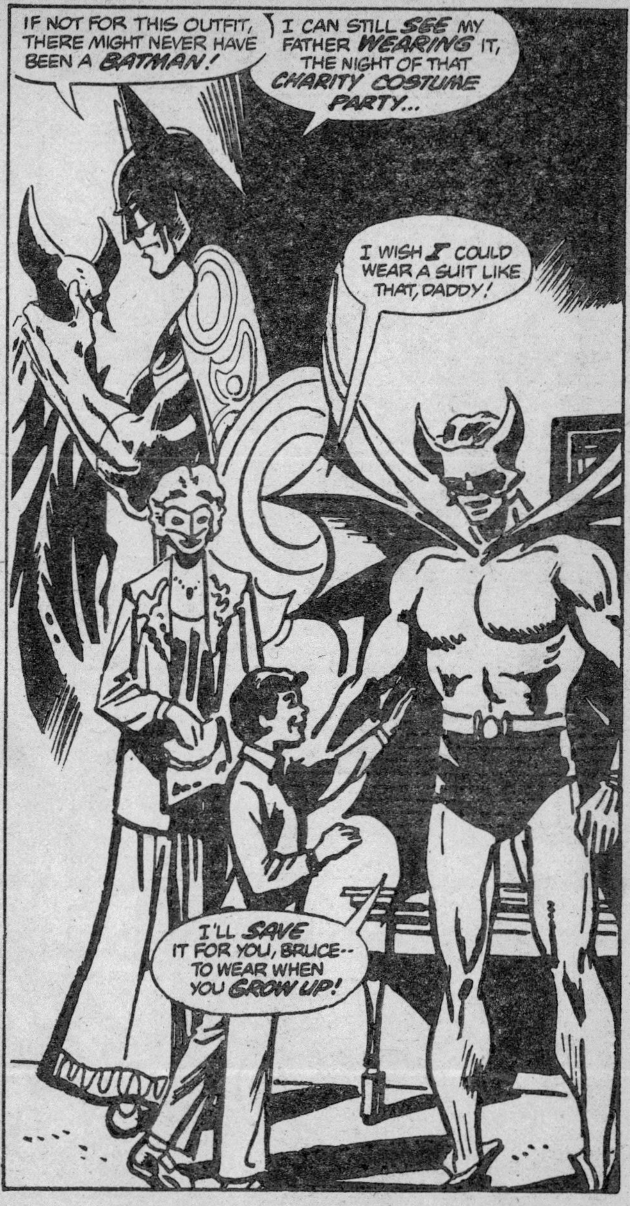
IF NOT FOR THIS OUTFIT, THERE MIGHT NEVER HAVE BEEN A BATMAN!
I CAN STILL SEE MY FATHER WEARING IT, THE NIGHT OF THAT CHARITY COSTUME PARTY...
I WISH I COULD WEAR A SUIT LIKE THAT, DADDY!
I'LL SAVE IT FOR YOU, BRUCE-- TO WEAR WHEN YOU GROW UP!

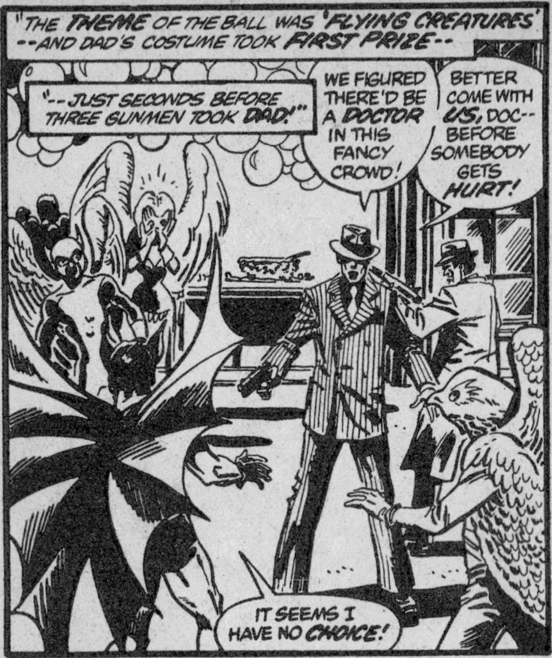
"THE THEME OF THE BALL WAS 'FLYING CREATURES' --AND DAD'S COSTUME TOOK FIRST PRIZE--
"--JUST SECONDS BEFORE THREE GUNMEN TOOK DAD!"
WE FIGURED THERE'D BE A DOCTOR IN THIS FANCY CROWD!
BETTER COME WITH US, DOC-- BEFORE SOMEBODY GETS HURT!
IT SEEMS I HAVE NO CHOICE!

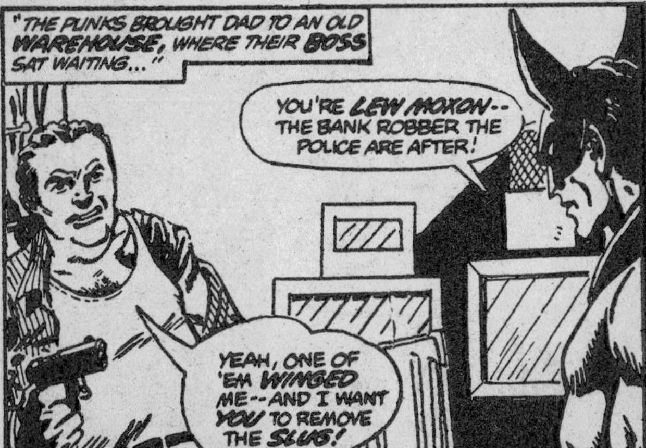
"THE PUNKS BROUGHT DAD TO AN OLD WAREHOUSE, WHERE THEIR BOSS SAT WAITING..."
YOU'RE LEW MOXON-- THE BANK ROBBER THE POLICE ARE AFTER!
YEAH, ONE OF 'EM WINGED ME--AND I WANT YOU TO REMOVE THE SLUG!

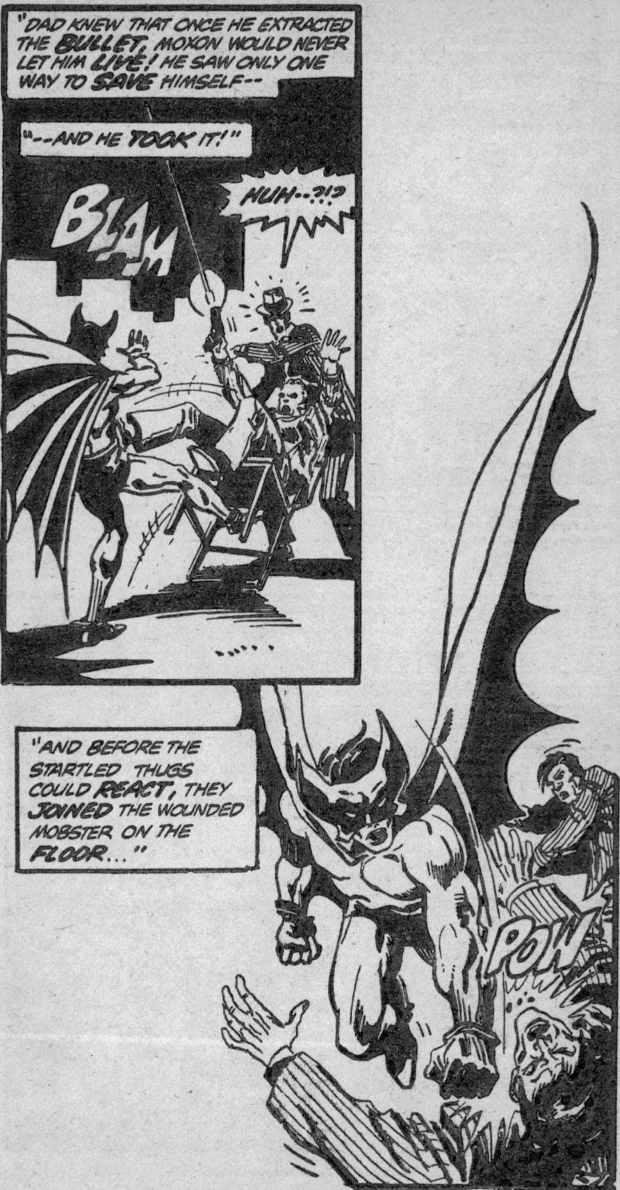
"DAD KNEW THAT ONCE HE EXTRACTED THE BULLET, MOXON WOULD NEVER LET HIM LIVE! HE SAW ONLY ONE WAY TO SAVE HIMSELF--
"--AND HE TOOK IT!"
BLAM
HUH--?!?
"AND BEFORE THE STARTLED THUGS COULD REACT, THEY JOINED THE WOUNDED MOBSTER ON THE FLOOR..."
POW

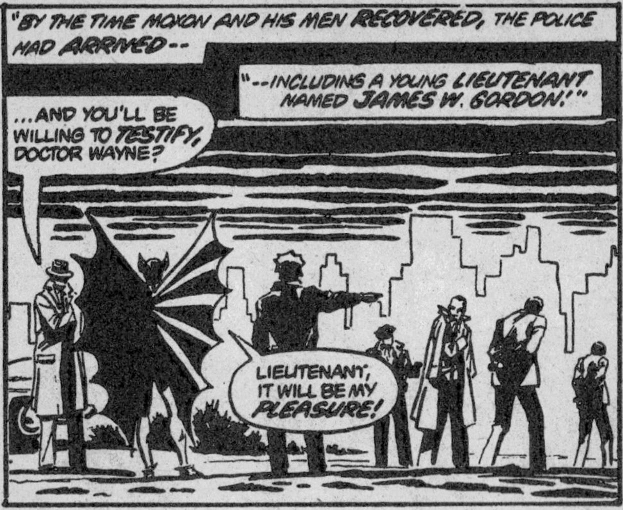
"BY THE TIME MOXON AND HIS MEN RECOVERED, THE POLICE HAD ARRIVED--
"--INCLUDING A YOUNG LIEUTENANT NAMED JAMES W. GORDON!"
...AND YOU'LL BE WILLING TO TESTIFY, DOCTOR WAYNE?
LIEUTENANT, IT WILL BE MY PLEASURE!

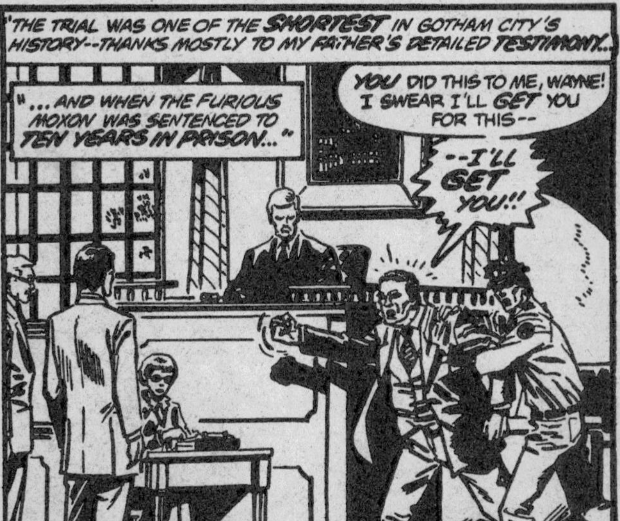
"THE TRIAL WAS ONE OF THE SHORTEST IN GOTHAM CITY'S HISTORY--THANKS MOSTLY TO MY FATHER'S DETAILED TESTIMONY...
"...AND WHEN THE FURIOUS MOXON WAS SENTENCED TO TEN YEARS IN PRISON..."
YOU DID THIS TO ME, WAYNE! I SWEAR I'LL GET YOU FOR THIS--
--I'LL GET YOU!!

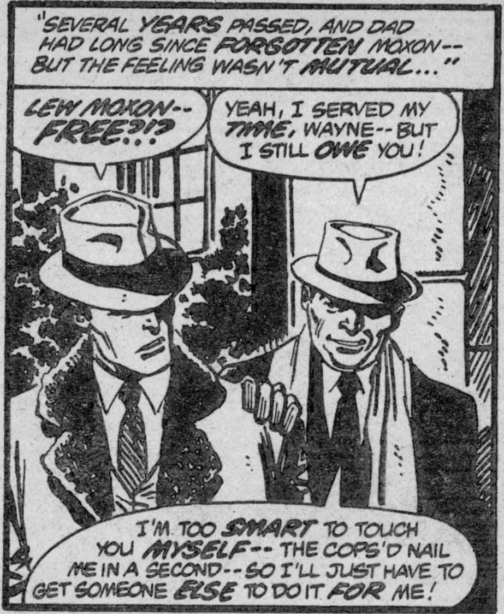
"SEVERAL YEARS PASSED, AND DAD HAD LONG SINCE FORGOTTEN MOXON-- BUT THE FEELING WASN'T MUTUAL..."
LEW MOXON-- FREE?!?
YEAH, I SERVED MY TIME, WAYNE-- BUT I STILL OWE YOU!
I'M TOO SMART TO TOUCH YOU MYSELF-- THE COPS'D NAIL ME IN A SECOND-- SO I'LL JUST HAVE TO GET SOMEONE ELSE TO DO IT FOR ME!

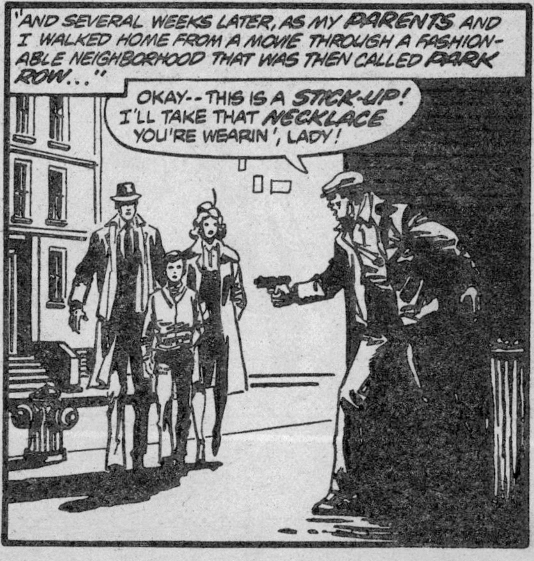
"AND SEVERAL WEEKS LATER, AS MY PARENTS AND I WALKED HOME FROM A MOVIE THROUGH A FASHION-ABLE NEIGHBORHOOD THAT WAS THEN CALLED PARK ROW..."
OKAY-- THIS IS A STICK-UP! I'LL TAKE THAT NECKLACE YOU'RE WEARIN', LADY!

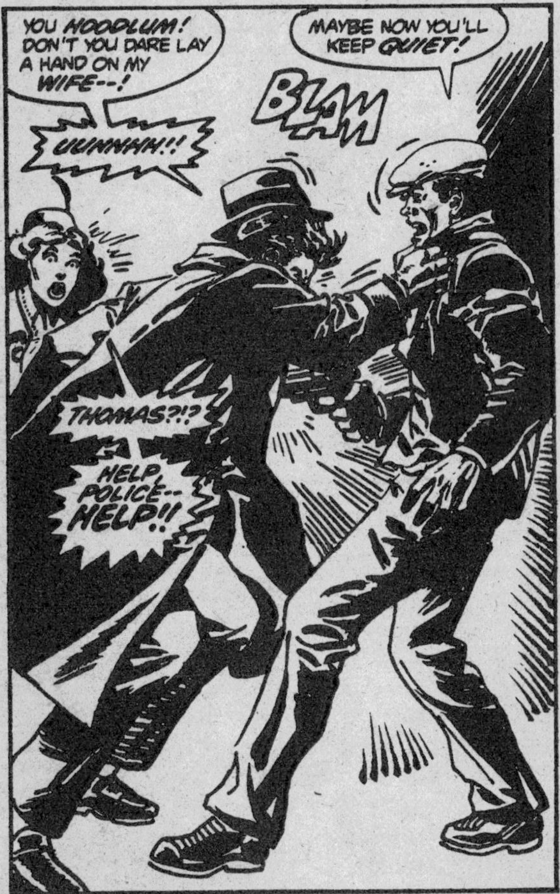
YOU HOODLUM! DON'T YOU DARE LAY A HAND ON MY WIFE--!
MAYBE NOW YOU'LL KEEP QUIET!
BLAM
UUNNHH!!
THOMAS?!?
HELP, POLICE-- HELP!!

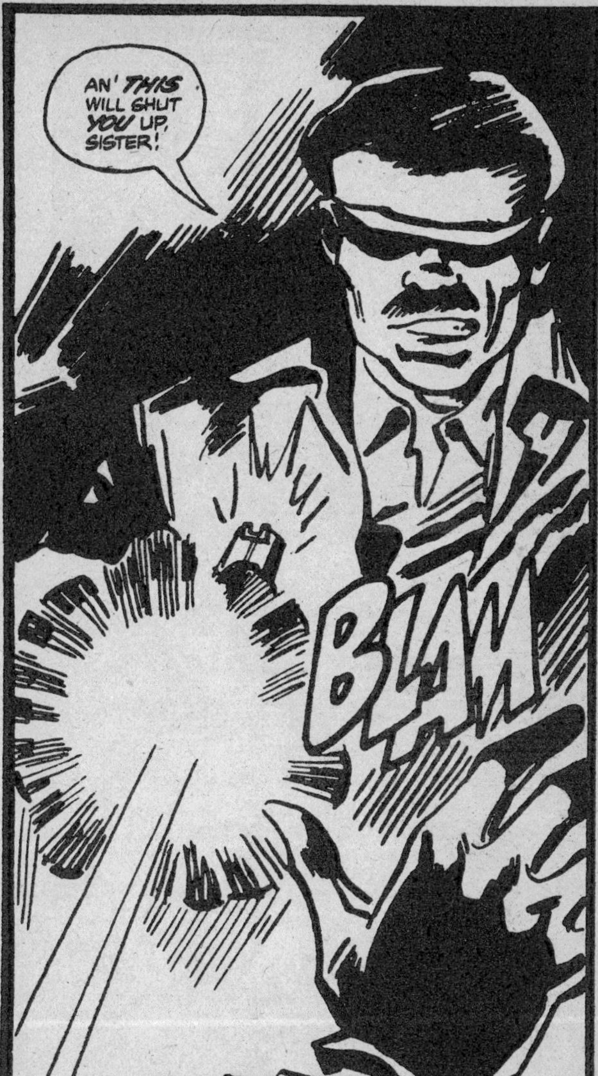
AN' THIS WILL SHUT YOU UP, SISTER!
BLAM

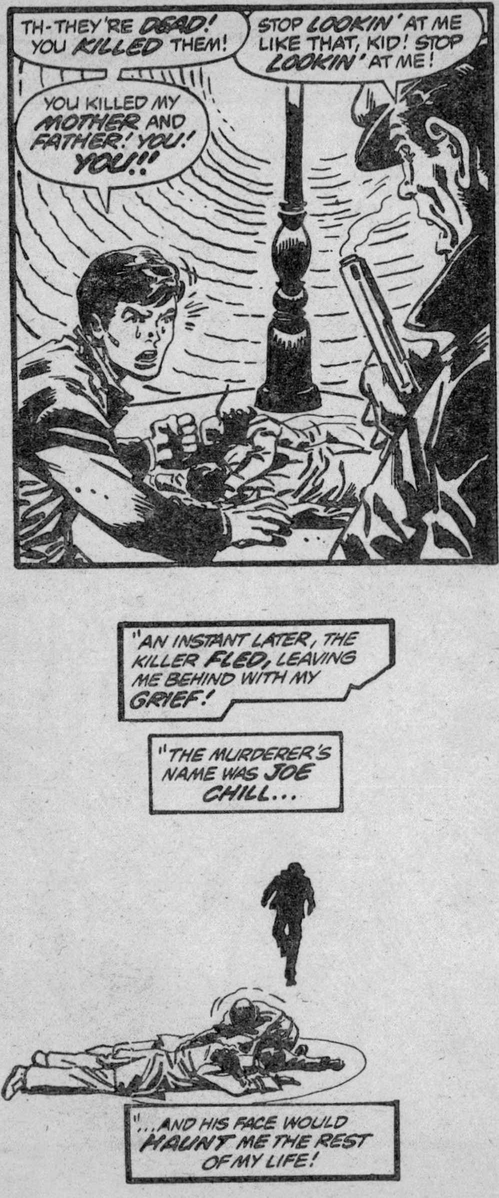
TH-THEY'RE DEAD! YOU KILLED THEM!
YOU KILLED MY MOTHER AND FATHER! YOU! YOU!!
STOP LOOKIN' AT ME LIKE THAT, KID! STOP LOOKIN' AT ME!
"AN INSTANT LATER, THE KILLER FLED, LEAVING ME BEHIND WITH MY GRIEF!
"THE MURDERER'S NAME WAS JOE CHILL...
"...AND HIS FACE WOULD HAUNT ME THE REST OF MY LIFE!

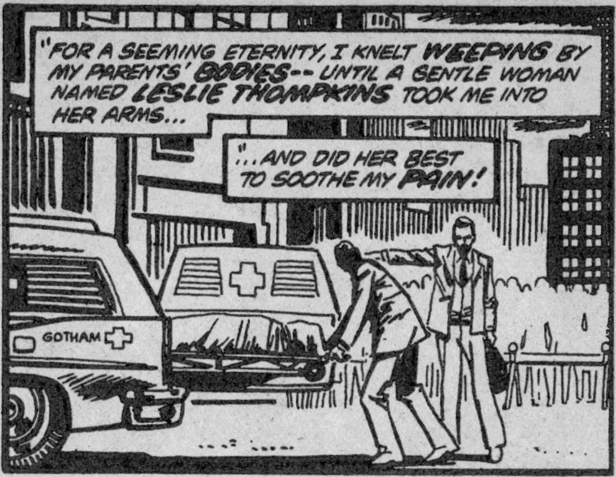
"FOR A SEEMING ETERNITY, I KNELT WEEPING BY MY PARENTS' BODIES-- UNTIL A GENTLE WOMAN NAMED LESLIE THOMPKINS TOOK ME INTO HER ARMS...
"...AND DID HER BEST TO SOOTHE MY PAIN!
GOTHAM

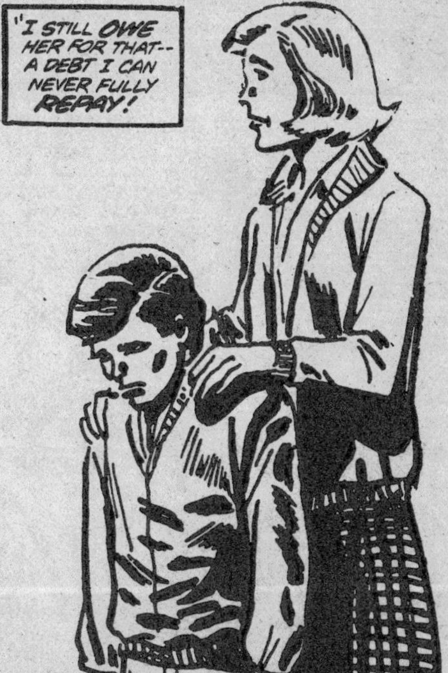
"I STILL OWE HER FOR THAT-- A DEBT I CAN NEVER FULLY REPAY!

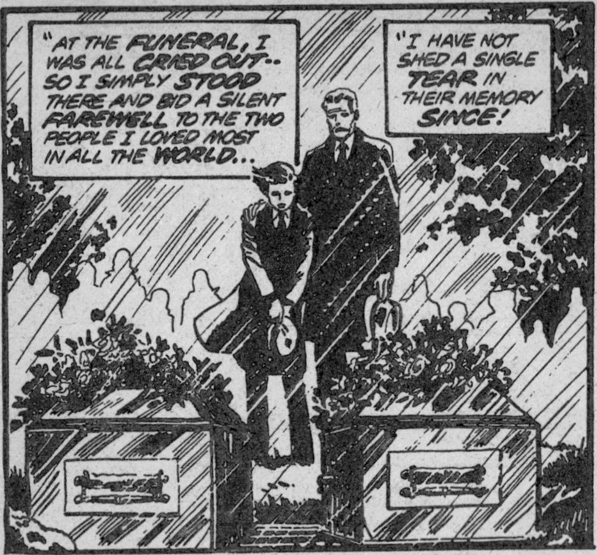
"AT THE FUNERAL, I WAS ALL CRIED OUT.. SO I SIMPLY STOOD THERE AND BID A SILENT FAREWELL TO THE TWO PEOPLE I LOVED MOST IN ALL THE WORLD...
"I HAVE NOT SHED A SINGLE TEAR IN THEIR MEMORY SINCE!

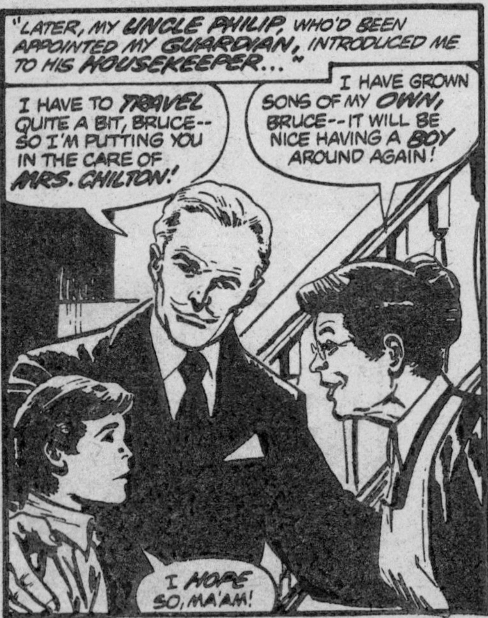
"LATER, MY UNCLE PHILIP, WHO'D BEEN APPOINTED MY GUARDIAN, INTRODUCED ME TO HIS HOUSEKEEPER..."
I HAVE TO TRAVEL QUITE A BIT, BRUCE-- SO I'M PUTTING YOU IN THE CARE OF MRS. CHILTON!
I HAVE GROWN SONS OF MY OWN, BRUCE--IT WILL BE NICE HAVING A BOY AROUND AGAIN!
I HOPE SO, MA'AM!

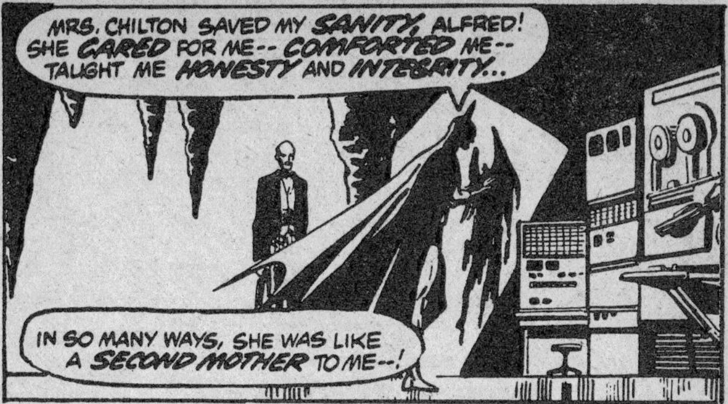
MRS. CHILTON SAVED MY SANITY, ALFRED! SHE CARED FOR ME-- COMFORTED ME-- TAUGHT ME HONESTY AND INTEGRITY...
IN SO MANY WAYS, SHE WAS LIKE A SECOND MOTHER TO ME--!

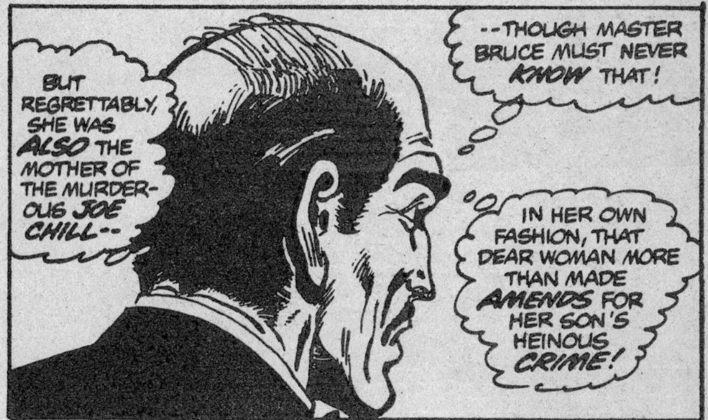
BUT REGRETTABLY, SHE WAS ALSO THE MOTHER OF THE MURDEROUS JOE CHILL--
--THOUGH MASTER BRUCE MUST NEVER KNOW THAT!
IN HER OWN FASHION, THAT DEAR WOMAN MORE THAN MADE AMENDS FOR HER SON'S HEINOUS CRIME!

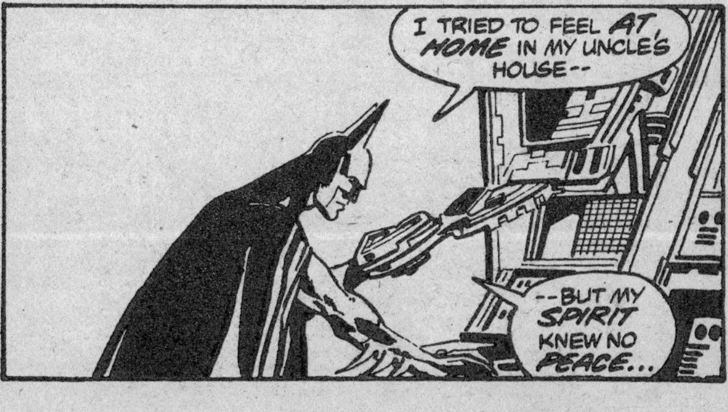
I TRIED TO FEEL AT HOME IN MY UNCLE'S HOUSE--
--BUT MY SPIRIT KNEW NO PEACE...

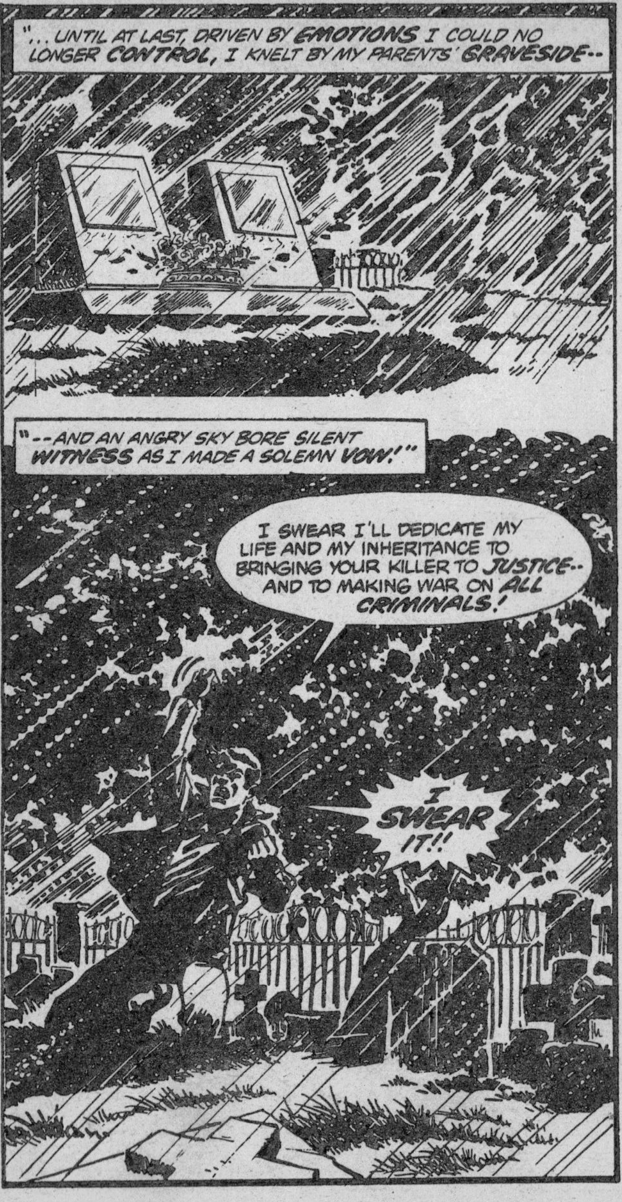
"...UNTIL AT LAST, DRIVEN BY EMOTIONS I COULD NO LONGER CONTROL, I KNELT BY MY PARENTS' GRAVESIDE--
"--AND AN ANGRY SKY BORE SILENT WITNESS AS I MADE A SOLEMN VOW!"
I SWEAR I'LL DEDICATE MY LIFE AND MY INHERITANCE TO BRINGING YOUR KILLER TO JUSTICE.. AND TO MAKING WAR ON ALL CRIMINALS!
I SWEAR IT!!

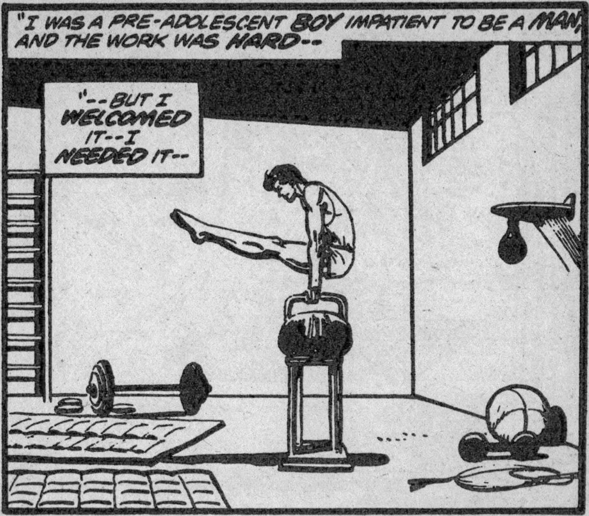
"I WAS A PRE-ADOLESCENT BOY IMPATIENT TO BE A MAN, AND THE WORK WAS HARD--
"--BUT I WELCOMED IT--I NEEDED IT--

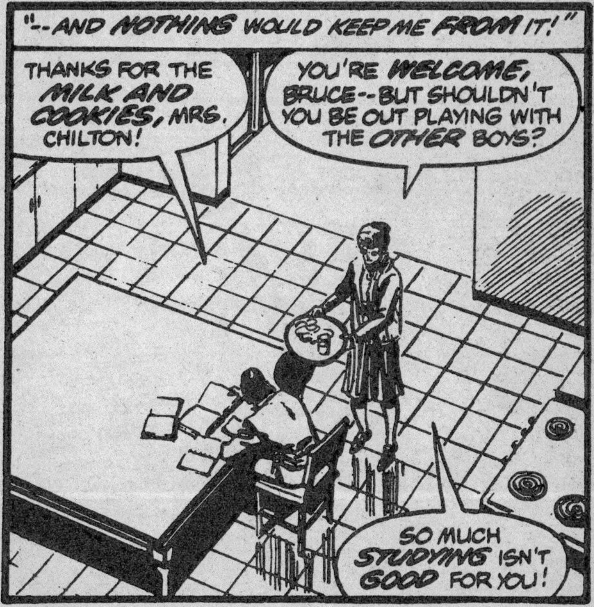
"--AND NOTHING WOULD KEEP ME FROM IT!"
THANKS FOR THE MILK AND COOKIES, MRS. CHILTON!
YOU'RE WELCOME, BRUCE--BUT SHOULDN'T YOU BE OUT PLAYING WITH THE OTHER BOYS?
SO MUCH STUDYING ISN'T GOOD FOR YOU!

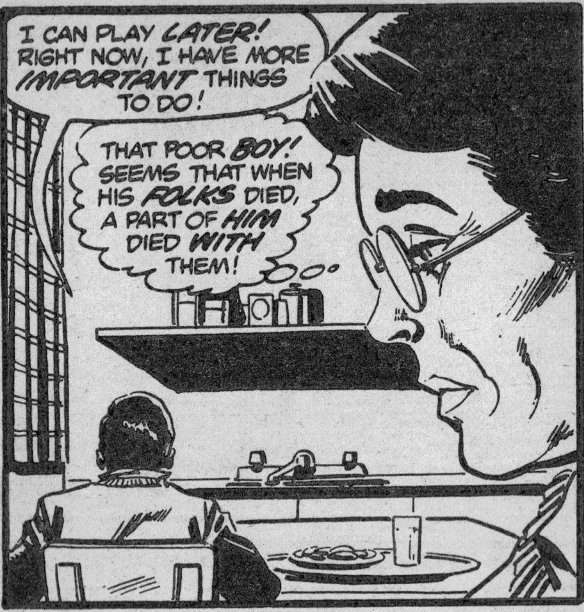
I CAN PLAY LATER! RIGHT NOW, I HAVE MORE IMPORTANT THINGS TO DO!
THAT POOR BOY! SEEMS THAT WHEN HIS FOLKS DIED, A PART OF HIM DIED WITH THEM!

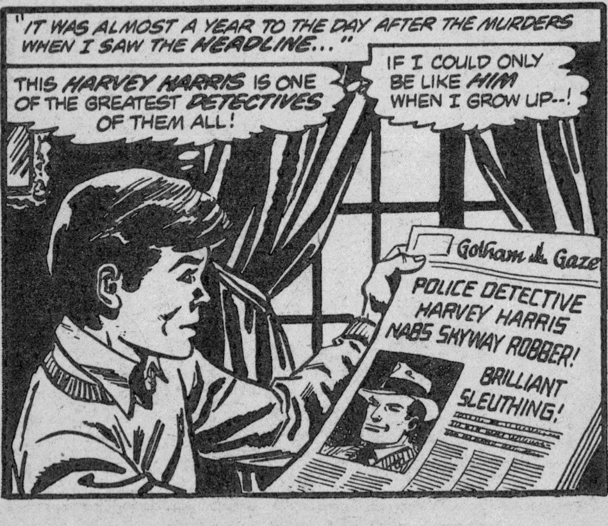
"IT WAS ALMOST A YEAR TO THE DAY AFTER THE MURDERS WHEN I SAW THE HEADLINE..."
THIS HARVEY HARRIS IS ONE OF THE GREATEST DETECTIVES OF THEM ALL!
IF I COULD ONLY BE LIKE HIM WHEN I GROW UP--!
Gotham Gaze
POLICE DETECTIVE HARVEY HARRIS NABS SKYWAY ROBBER!
BRILLIANT SLEUTHING!

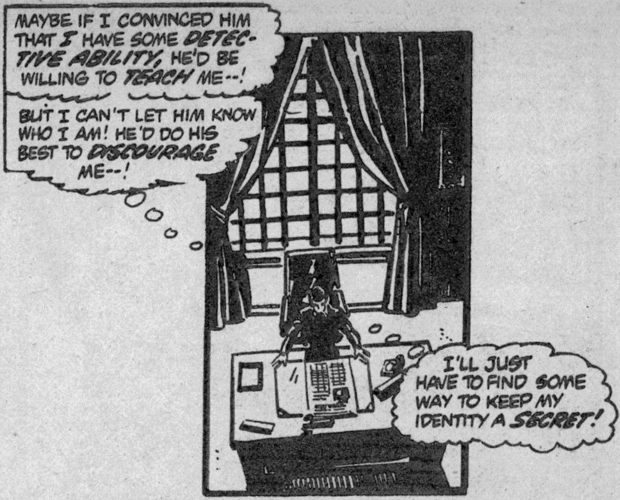
MAYBE IF I CONVINCED HIM THAT I HAVE SOME DETECTIVE ABILITY, HE'D BE WILLING TO TEACH ME--!
BUT I CAN'T LET HIM KNOW WHO I AM! HE'D DO HIS BEST TO DISCOURAGE ME--!
I'LL JUST HAVE TO FIND SOME WAY TO KEEP MY IDENTITY A SECRET!

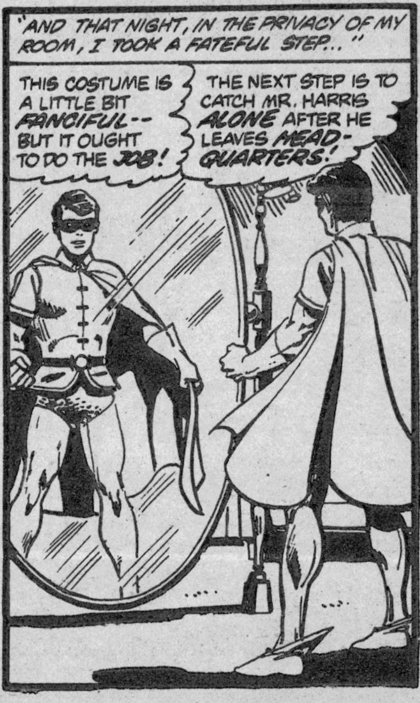
"AND THAT NIGHT, IN THE PRIVACY OF MY ROOM, I TOOK A FATEFUL STEP..."
THIS COSTUME IS A LITTLE BIT FANCIFUL-- BUT IT OUGHT TO DO THE JOB!
THE NEXT STEP IS TO CATCH MR. HARRIS ALONE AFTER HE LEAVES HEAD-QUARTERS!

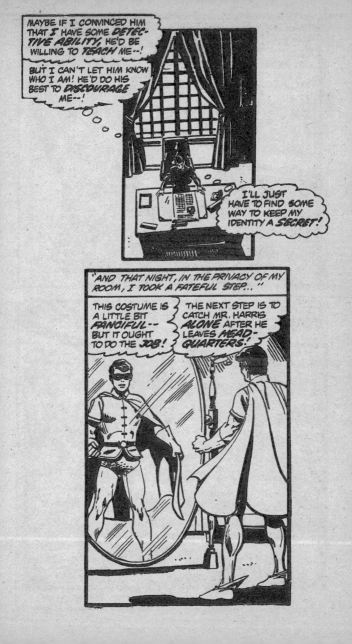

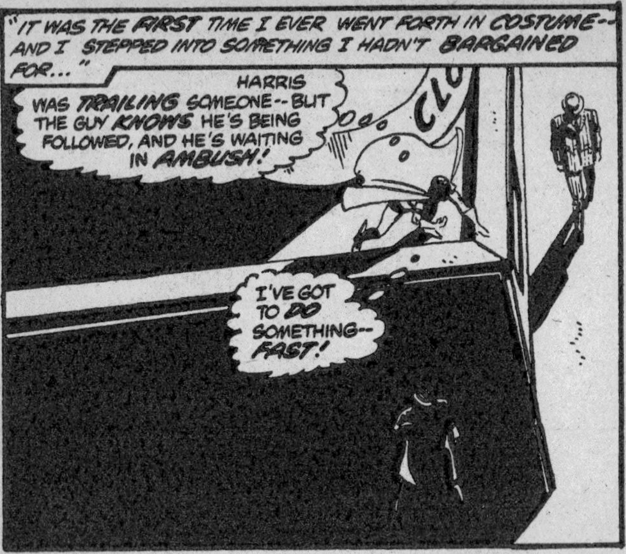
"IT WAS THE FIRST TIME I EVER WENT FORTH IN COSTUME--AND I STEPPED INTO SOMETHING I HADN'T BARGAINED FOR..."
HARRIS WAS TRAILING SOMEONE--BUT THE GUY KNOWS HE'S BEING FOLLOWED, AND HE'S WAITING IN AMBUSH!
I'VE GOT TO DO SOMETHING--FAST!

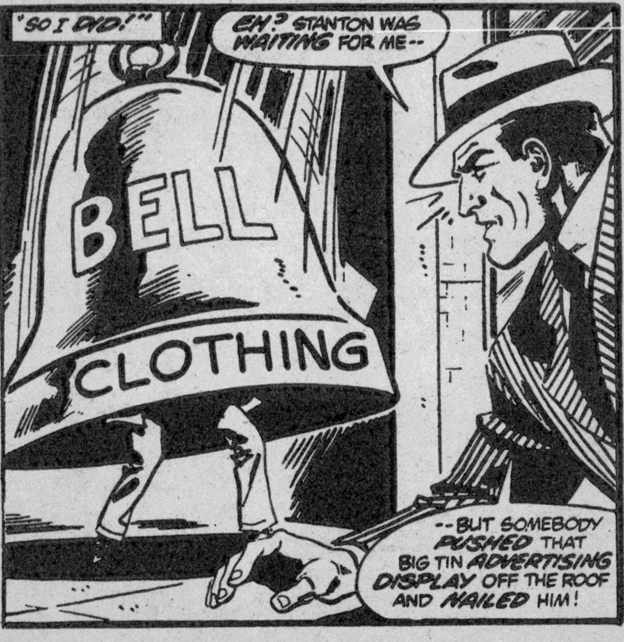
"SO I DID!"
EH? STANTON WAS WAITING FOR ME--
BELL
CLOTHING
--BUT SOMEBODY PUSHED THAT BIG TIN ADVERTISING DISPLAY OFF THE ROOF AND NAILED HIM!

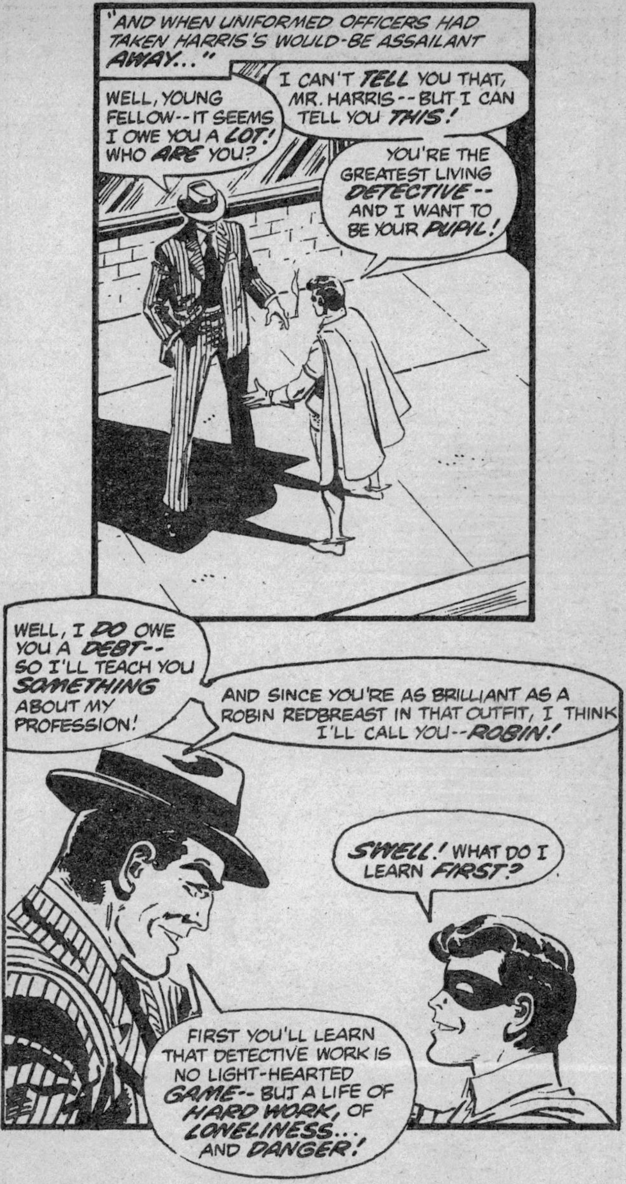
"AND WHEN UNIFORMED OFFICERS HAD TAKEN HARRIS'S WOULD-BE ASSAILANT AWAY..."
WELL, YOUNG FELLOW--IT SEEMS I OWE YOU A LOT! WHO ARE YOU?
I CAN'T TELL YOU THAT, MR. HARRIS--BUT I CAN TELL YOU THIS!
YOU'RE THE GREATEST LIVING DETECTIVE--AND I WANT TO BE YOUR PUPIL!
WELL, I DO OWE YOU A DEBT--SO I'LL TEACH YOU SOMETHING ABOUT MY PROFESSION!
AND SINCE YOU'RE AS BRILLIANT AS A ROBIN REDBREAST IN THAT OUTFIT, I THINK I'LL CALL YOU--ROBIN!
SWELL! WHAT DO I LEARN FIRST?
FIRST YOU'LL LEARN THAT DETECTIVE WORK IS NO LIGHT-HEARTED GAME--BUT A LIFE OF HARD WORK, OF LONELINESS... AND DANGER!

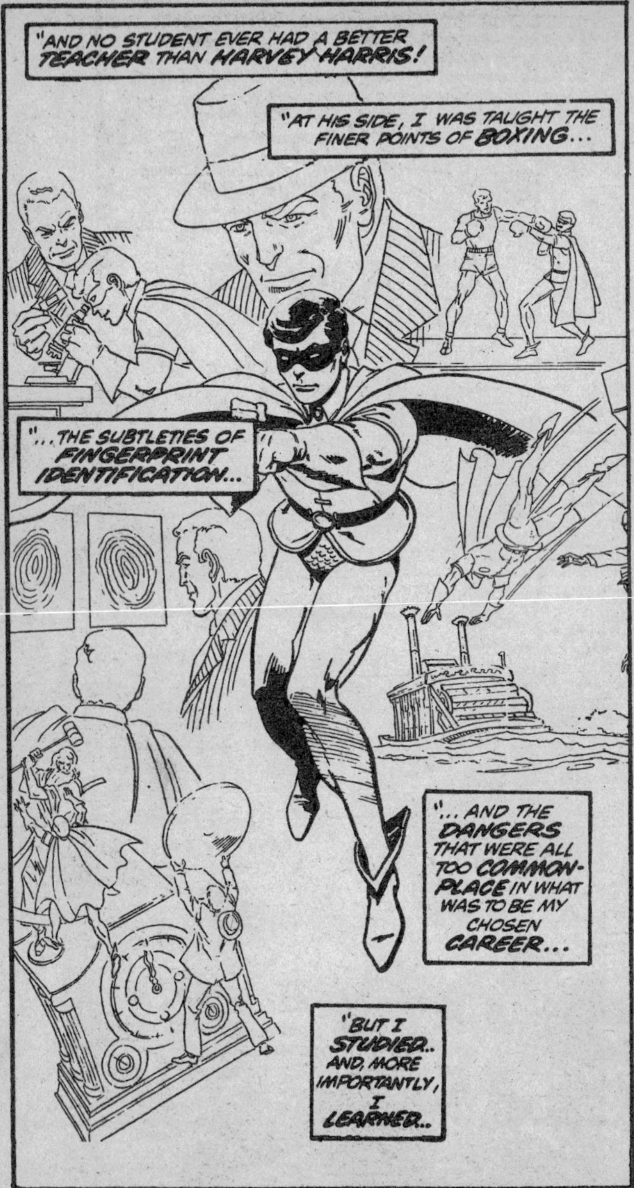
"AND NO STUDENT EVER HAD A BETTER TEACHER THAN HARVEY HARRIS!
"AT HIS SIDE, I WAS TAUGHT THE FINER POINTS OF BOXING...
"...THE SUBTLETIES OF FINGERPRINT IDENTIFICATION...
"...AND THE DANGERS THAT WERE ALL TOO COMMON-PLACE IN WHAT WAS TO BE MY CHOSEN CAREER...
"BUT I STUDIED.. AND, MORE IMPORTANTLY, I LEARNED..

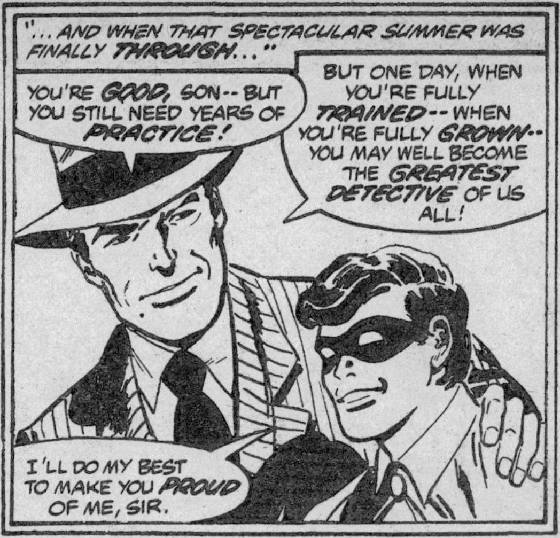
"... AND WHEN THAT SPECTACULAR SUMMER WAS FINALLY THROUGH..."
YOU'RE GOOD, SON-- BUT YOU STILL NEED YEARS OF PRACTICE!
BUT ONE DAY, WHEN YOU'RE FULLY TRAINED-- WHEN YOU'RE FULLY GROWN-- YOU MAY WELL BECOME THE GREATEST DETECTIVE OF US ALL!
I'LL DO MY BEST TO MAKE YOU PROUD OF ME, SIR.

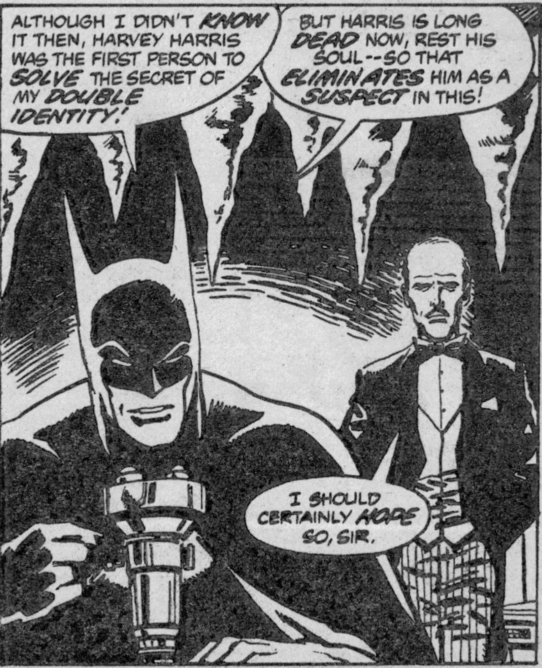
ALTHOUGH I DIDN'T KNOW IT THEN, HARVEY HARRIS WAS THE FIRST PERSON TO SOLVE THE SECRET OF MY DOUBLE IDENTITY!
BUT HARRIS IS LONG DEAD NOW, REST HIS SOUL--SO THAT ELIMINATES HIM AS A SUSPECT IN THIS!
I SHOULD CERTAINLY HOPE SO, SIR.

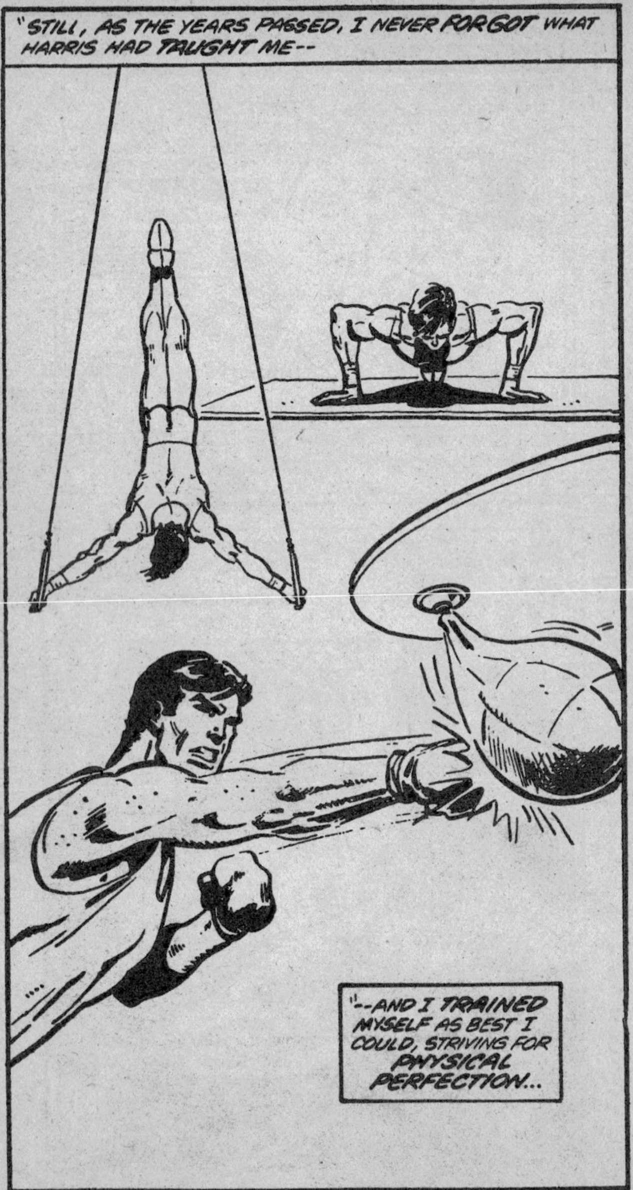
"STILL, AS THE YEARS PASSED, I NEVER FORGOT WHAT HARRIS HAD TAUGHT ME--
"--AND I TRAINED MYSELF AS BEST I COULD, STRIVING FOR PHYSICAL PERFECTION...

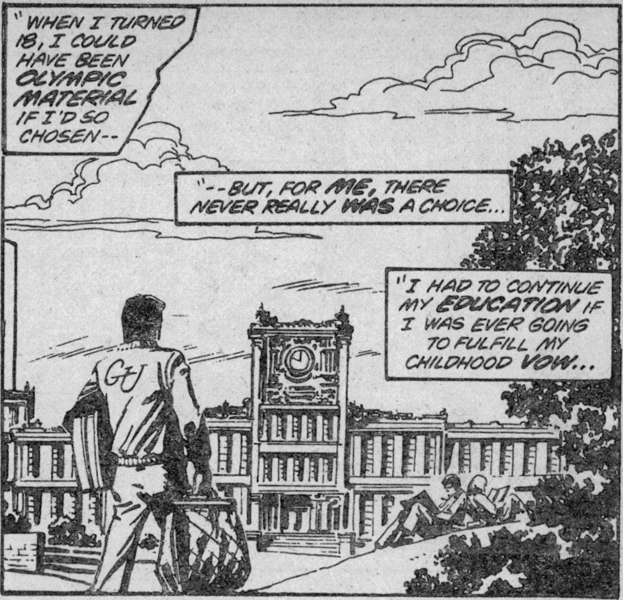
"WHEN I TURNED 18, I COULD HAVE BEEN OLYMPIC MATERIAL IF I'D SO CHOSEN--
"--BUT, FOR ME, THERE NEVER REALLY WAS A CHOICE...
"I HAD TO CONTINUE MY EDUCATION IF I WAS EVER GOING TO FULFILL MY CHILDHOOD VOW...

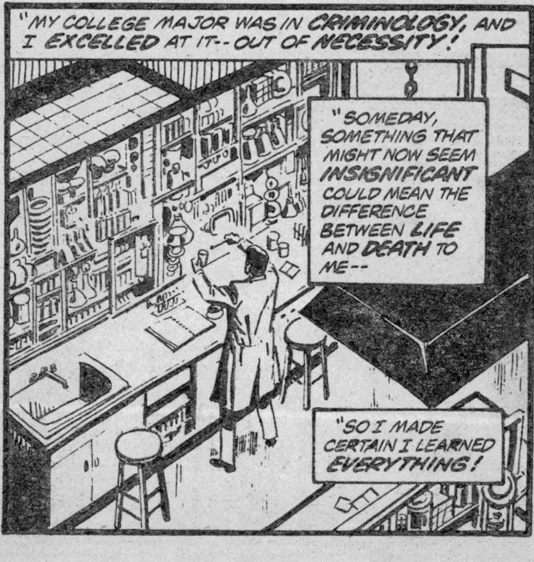
"MY COLLEGE MAJOR WAS IN CRIMINOLOGY, AND I EXCELLED AT IT--OUT OF NECESSITY!
"SOMEDAY, SOMETHING THAT MIGHT NOW SEEM INSIGNIFICANT COULD MEAN THE DIFFERENCE BETWEEN LIFE AND DEATH TO ME--
"SO I MADE CERTAIN I LEARNED EVERYTHING!

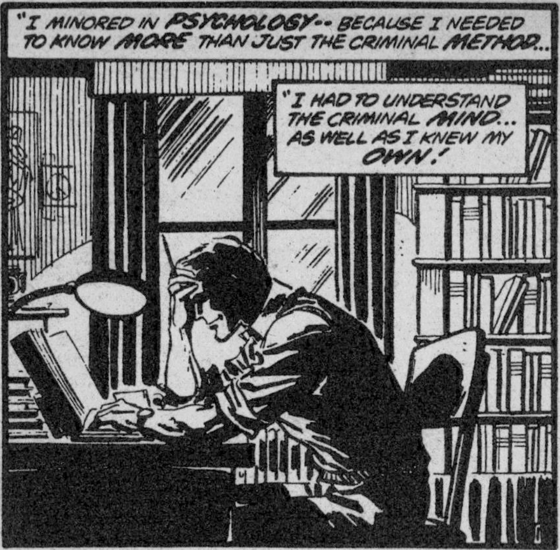
"I MINORED IN PSYCHOLOGY-- BECAUSE I NEEDED TO KNOW MORE THAN JUST THE CRIMINAL METHOD...
"I HAD TO UNDERSTAND THE CRIMINAL MIND... AS WELL AS I KNEW MY OWN!

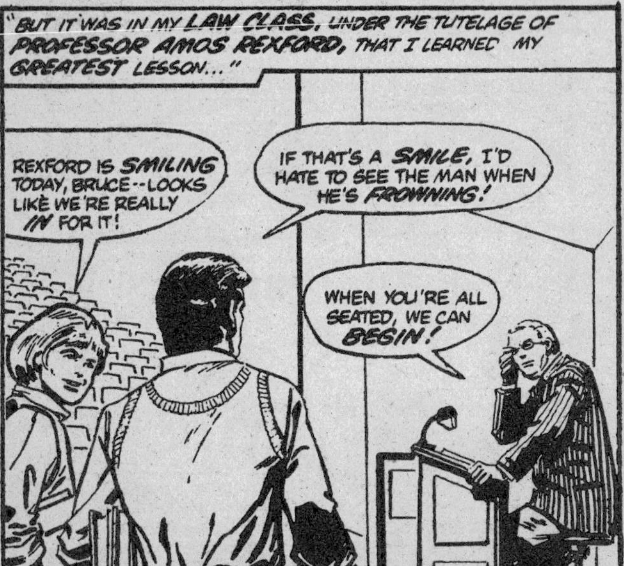
"BUT IT WAS IN MY LAW CLASS, UNDER THE TUTELAGE OF PROFESSOR AMOS REXFORD, THAT I LEARNED MY GREATEST LESSON..."
REXFORD IS SMILING TODAY, BRUCE--LOOKS LIKE WE'RE REALLY IN FOR IT!
IF THAT'S A SMILE, I'D HATE TO SEE THE MAN WHEN HE'S FROWNING!
WHEN YOU'RE ALL SEATED, WE CAN BEGIN!

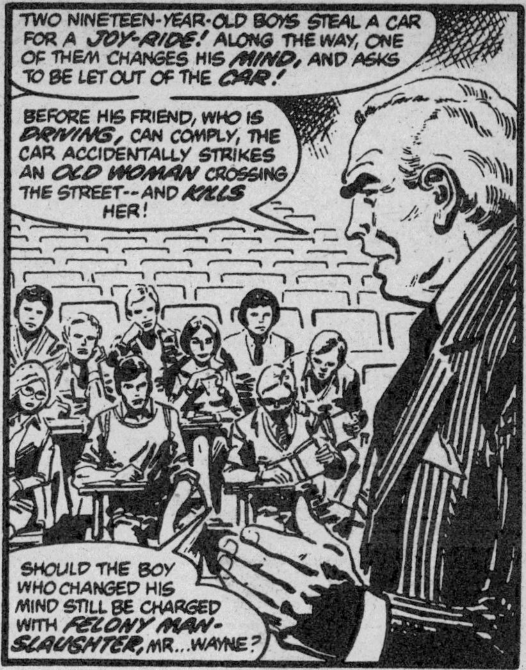
TWO NINETEEN-YEAR-OLD BOYS STEAL A CAR FOR A JOY-RIDE! ALONG THE WAY, ONE OF THEM CHANGES HIS MIND, AND ASKS TO BE LET OUT OF THE CAR!
BEFORE HIS FRIEND, WHO IS DRIVING, CAN COMPLY, THE CAR ACCIDENTALLY STRIKES AN OLD WOMAN CROSSING THE STREET--AND KILLS HER!
SHOULD THE BOY WHO CHANGED HIS MIND STILL BE CHARGED WITH FELONY MANSLAUGHTER, MR...WAYNE?

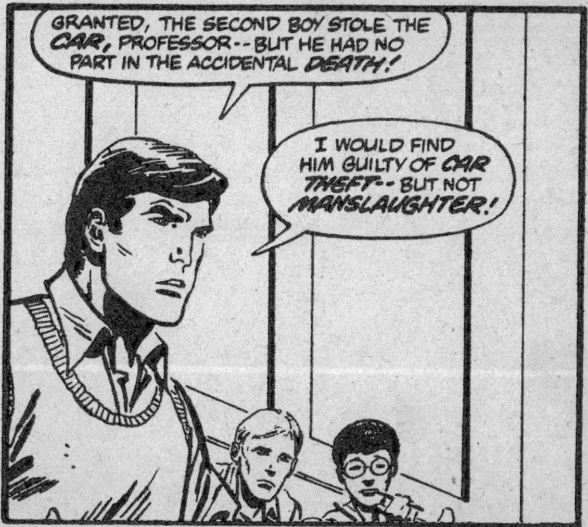
GRANTED, THE SECOND BOY STOLE THE CAR, PROFESSOR--BUT HE HAD NO PART IN THE ACCIDENTAL DEATH!
I WOULD FIND HIM GUILTY OF CAR THEFT--BUT NOT MANSLAUGHTER!

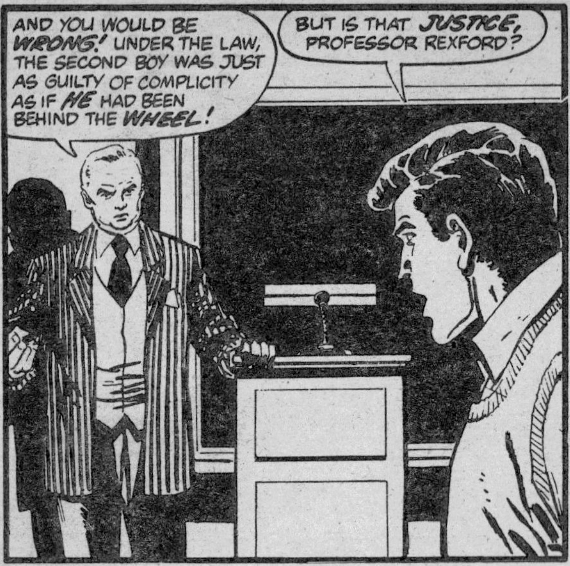
AND YOU WOULD BE WRONG! UNDER THE LAW, THE SECOND BOY WAS JUST AS GUILTY OF COMPLICITY AS IF HE HAD BEEN BEHIND THE WHEEL!
BUT IS THAT JUSTICE, PROFESSOR REXFORD?

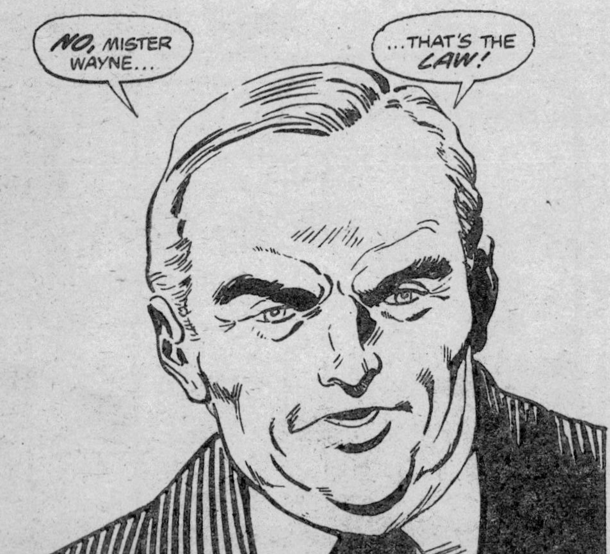
NO, MISTER WAYNE...
...THAT'S THE LAW!

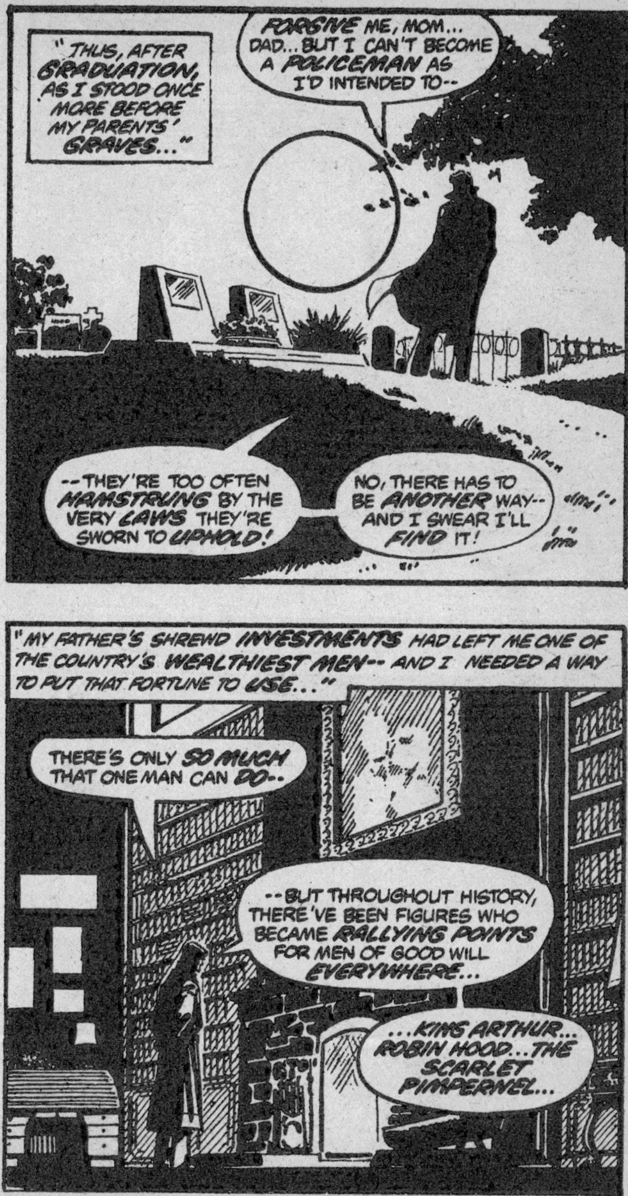
"THUS, AFTER GRADUATION, AS I STOOD ONCE MORE BEFORE MY PARENTS' GRAVES..."
FORGIVE ME, MOM... DAD... BUT I CAN'T BECOME A POLICEMAN AS I'D INTENDED TO--
--THEY'RE TOO OFTEN HAMSTRUNG BY THE VERY LAWS THEY'RE SWORN TO UPHOLD!
NO, THERE HAS TO BE ANOTHER WAY-- AND I SWEAR I'LL FIND IT!
"MY FATHER'S SHREWD INVESTMENTS HAD LEFT ME ONE OF THE COUNTRY'S WEALTHIEST MEN-- AND I NEEDED A WAY TO PUT THAT FORTUNE TO USE..."
THERE'S ONLY SO MUCH THAT ONE MAN CAN DO--
--BUT THROUGHOUT HISTORY, THERE'VE BEEN FIGURES WHO BECAME RALLYING POINTS FOR MEN OF GOOD WILL EVERYWHERE...
...KING ARTHUR... ROBIN HOOD... THE SCARLET PIMPERNEL...

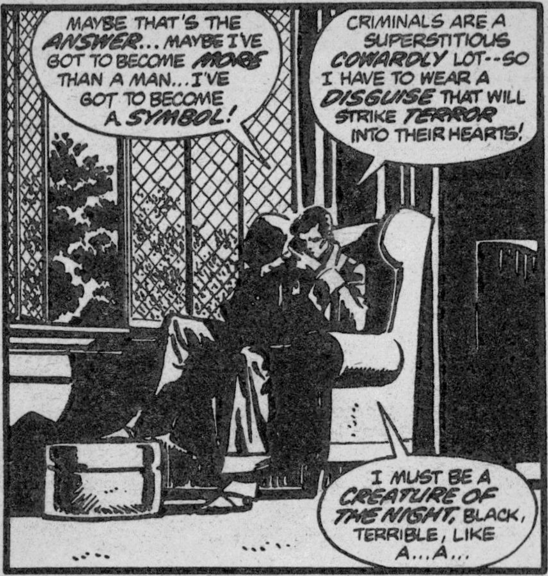
MAYBE THAT'S THE ANSWER... MAYBE I'VE GOT TO BECOME MORE THAN A MAN... I'VE GOT TO BECOME A SYMBOL!
CRIMINALS ARE A SUPERSTITIOUS COWARDLY LOT--SO I HAVE TO WEAR A DISGUISE THAT WILL STRIKE TERROR INTO THEIR HEARTS!
I MUST BE A CREATURE OF THE NIGHT, BLACK, TERRIBLE, LIKE A...A...

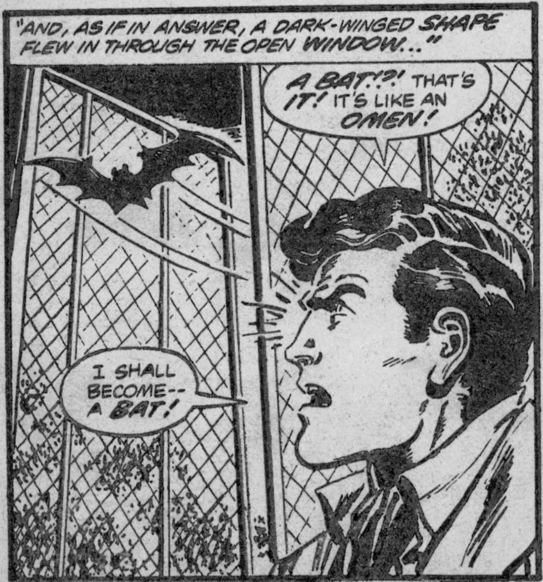
"AND, AS IF IN ANSWER, A DARK-WINGED SHAPE FLEW IN THROUGH THE OPEN WINDOW..."
A BAT!?! THAT'S IT! IT'S LIKE AN OMEN!
I SHALL BECOME-- A BAT!

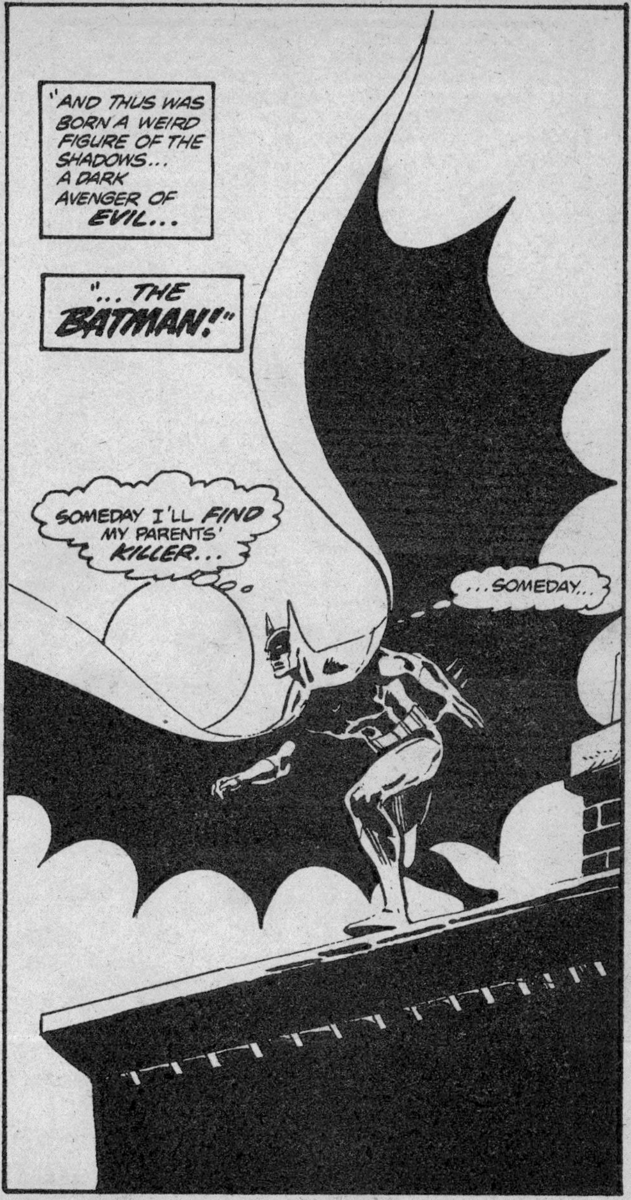
"AND THUS WAS BORN A WEIRD FIGURE OF THE SHADOWS... A DARK AVENGER OF EVIL...
"... THE BATMAN!"
SOMEDAY I'LL FIND MY PARENTS' KILLER...
...SOMEDAY...

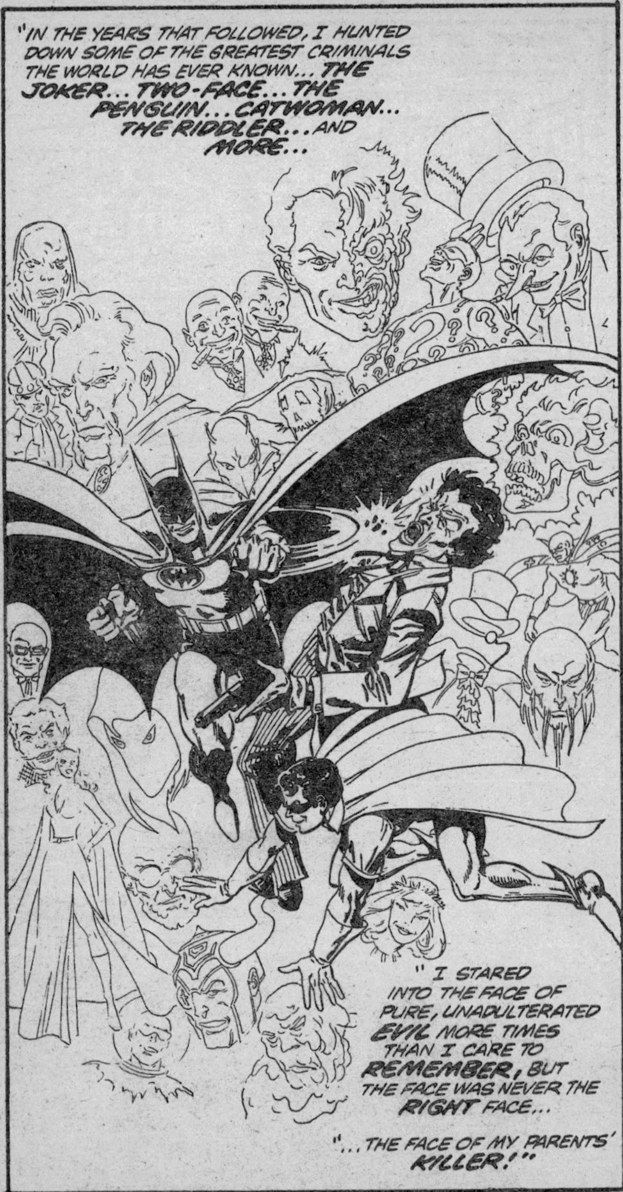
"IN THE YEARS THAT FOLLOWED, I HUNTED DOWN SOME OF THE GREATEST CRIMINALS THE WORLD HAS EVER KNOWN... THE JOKER... TWO-FACE... THE PENGUIN... CATWOMAN... THE RIDDLER... AND MORE...
"I STARED INTO THE FACE OF PURE, UNADULTERATED EVIL MORE TIMES THAN I CARE TO REMEMBER, BUT THE FACE WAS NEVER THE RIGHT FACE...
"... THE FACE OF MY PARENTS' KILLER!"

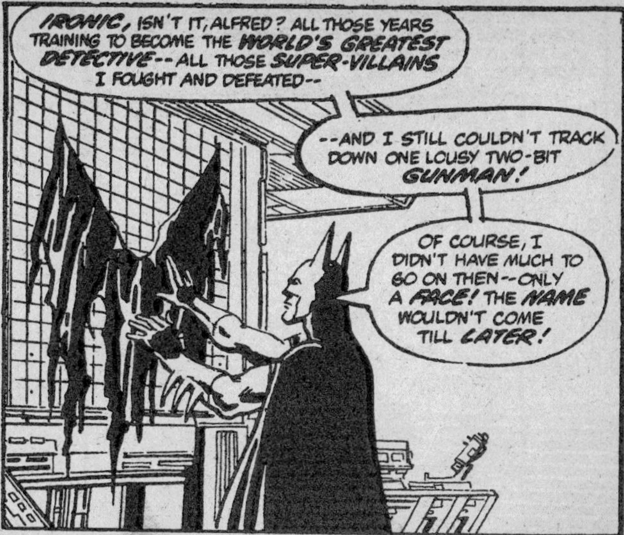
IRONIC, ISN'T IT, ALFRED? ALL THOSE YEARS TRAINING TO BECOME THE WORLD'S GREATEST DETECTIVE--ALL THOSE SUPER-VILLAINS I FOUGHT AND DEFEATED--
--AND I STILL COULDN'T TRACK DOWN ONE LOUSY TWO-BIT GUNMAN!
OF COURSE, I DIDN'T HAVE MUCH TO GO ON THEN--ONLY A FACE! THE NAME WOULDN'T COME TILL LATER!

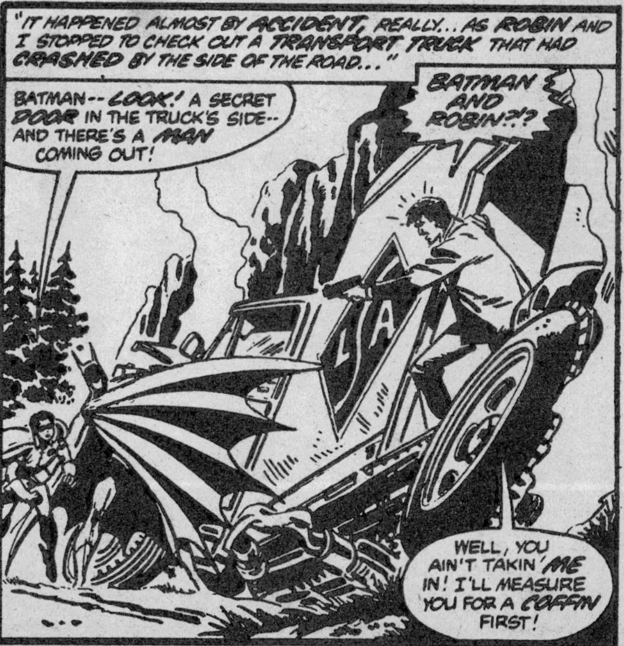
"IT HAPPENED ALMOST BY ACCIDENT, REALLY... AS ROBIN AND I STOPPED TO CHECK OUT A TRANSPORT TRUCK THAT HAD CRASHED BY THE SIDE OF THE ROAD..."
BATMAN--LOOK! A SECRET DOOR IN THE TRUCK'S SIDE--AND THERE'S A MAN COMING OUT!
BATMAN AND ROBIN?!?
WELL, YOU AIN'T TAKIN' ME IN! I'LL MEASURE YOU FOR A COFFIN FIRST!

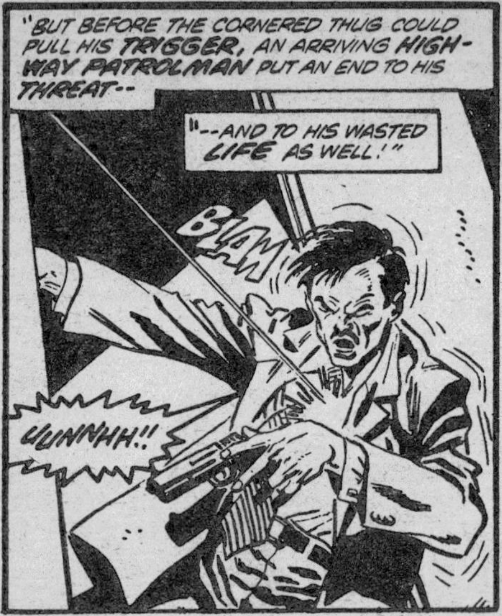
"BUT BEFORE THE CORNERED THUG COULD PULL HIS TRIGGER, AN ARRIVING HIGH-WAY PATROLMAN PUT AN END TO HIS THREAT--
"--AND TO HIS WASTED LIFE AS WELL!"
BLAM
UUNNHH!!

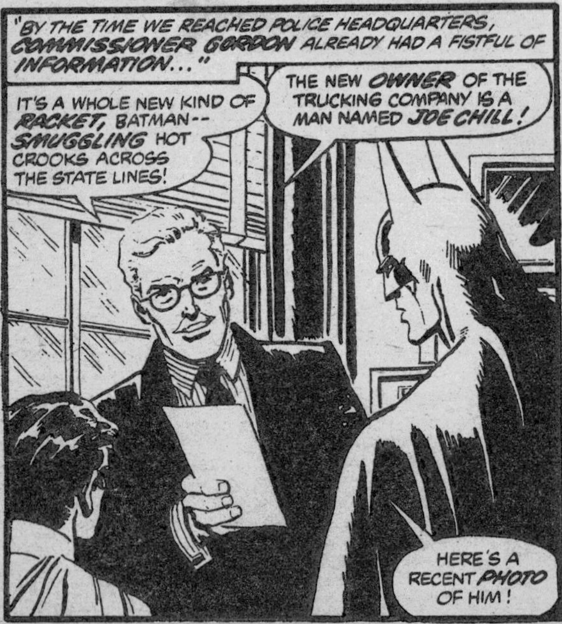
"BY THE TIME WE REACHED POLICE HEADQUARTERS, COMMISSIONER GORDON ALREADY HAD A FISTFUL OF INFORMATION..."
IT'S A WHOLE NEW KIND OF RACKET, BATMAN-- SMUGGLING HOT CROOKS ACROSS THE STATE LINES!
THE NEW OWNER OF THE TRUCKING COMPANY IS A MAN NAMED JOE CHILL!
HERE'S A RECENT PHOTO OF HIM!

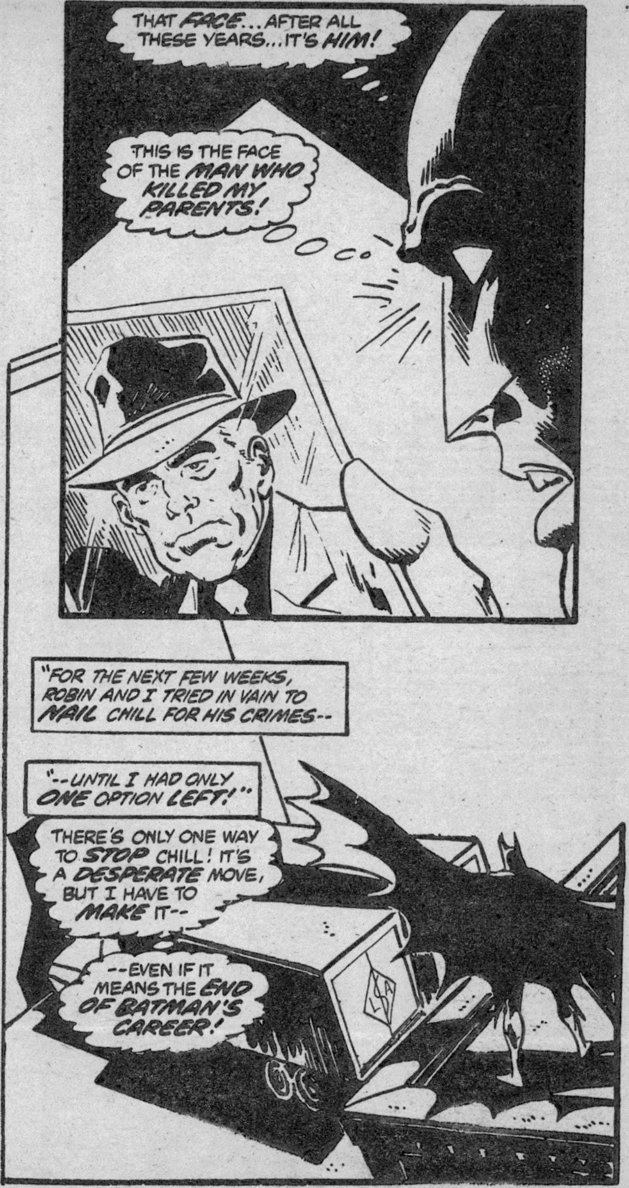
THAT FACE... AFTER ALL THESE YEARS... IT'S HIM!
THIS IS THE FACE OF THE MAN WHO KILLED MY PARENTS!
"FOR THE NEXT FEW WEEKS, ROBIN AND I TRIED IN VAIN TO NAIL CHILL FOR HIS CRIMES--
"--UNTIL I HAD ONLY ONE OPTION LEFT!"
THERE'S ONLY ONE WAY TO STOP CHILL! IT'S A DESPERATE MOVE, BUT I HAVE TO MAKE IT--
--EVEN IF IT MEANS THE END OF BATMAN'S CAREER!

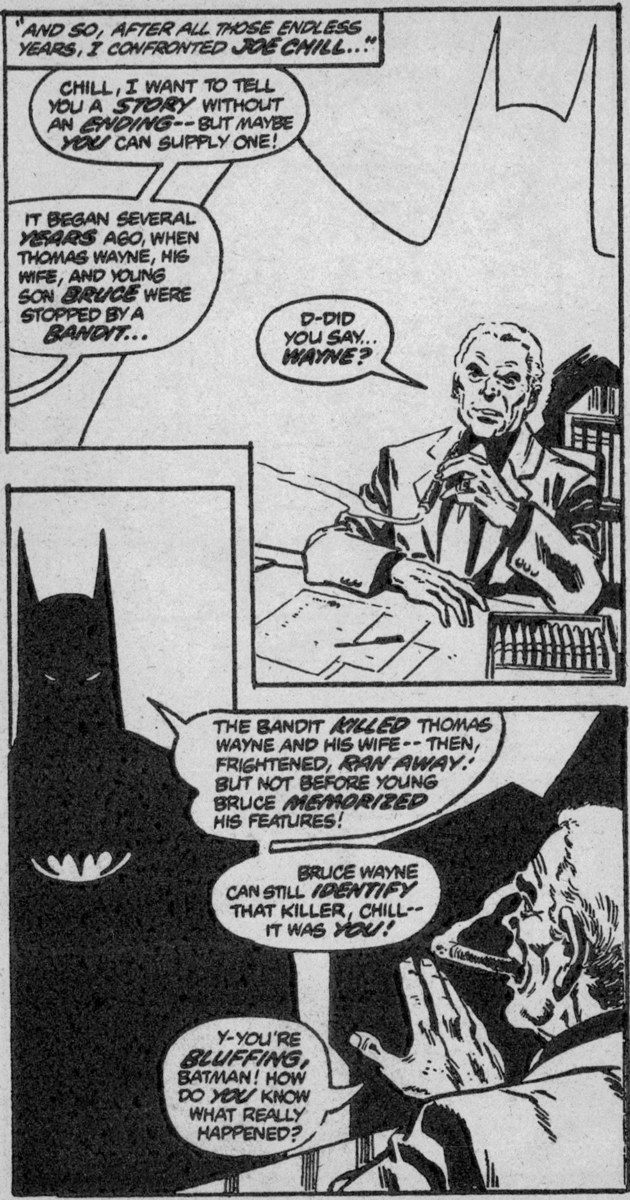
"AND SO, AFTER ALL THOSE ENDLESS YEARS, I CONFRONTED JOE CHILL..."
CHILL, I WANT TO TELL YOU A STORY WITHOUT AN ENDING-- BUT MAYBE YOU CAN SUPPLY ONE!
IT BEGAN SEVERAL YEARS AGO, WHEN THOMAS WAYNE, HIS WIFE, AND YOUNG SON BRUCE WERE STOPPED BY A BANDIT...
D-DID YOU SAY... WAYNE?
THE BANDIT KILLED THOMAS WAYNE AND HIS WIFE-- THEN, FRIGHTENED, RAN AWAY! BUT NOT BEFORE YOUNG BRUCE MEMORIZED HIS FEATURES!
BRUCE WAYNE CAN STILL IDENTIFY THAT KILLER, CHILL-- IT WAS YOU!
Y-YOU'RE BLUFFING, BATMAN! HOW DO YOU KNOW WHAT REALLY HAPPENED?

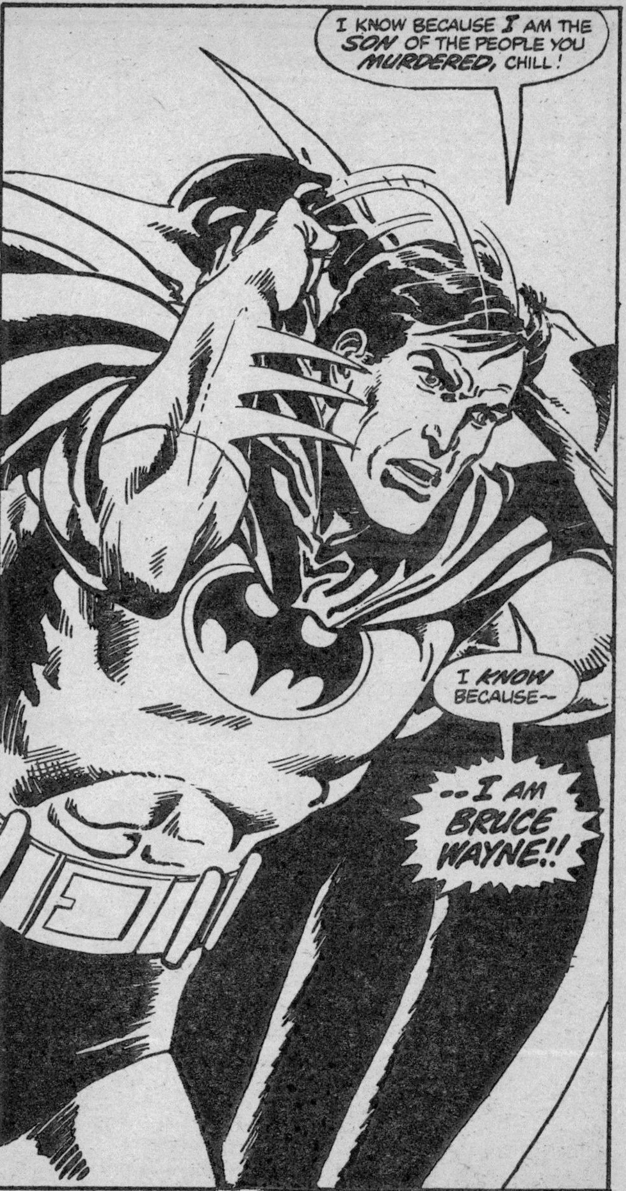
I KNOW BECAUSE I AM THE SON OF THE PEOPLE YOU MURDERED, CHILL!
I KNOW BECAUSE--
..I AM BRUCE WAYNE!!

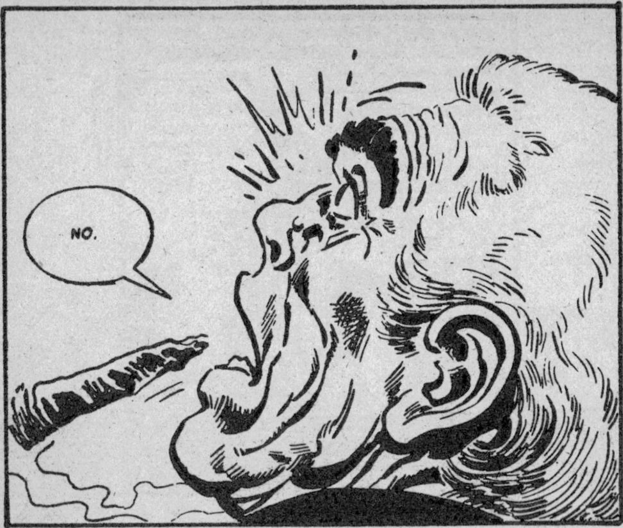
NO.

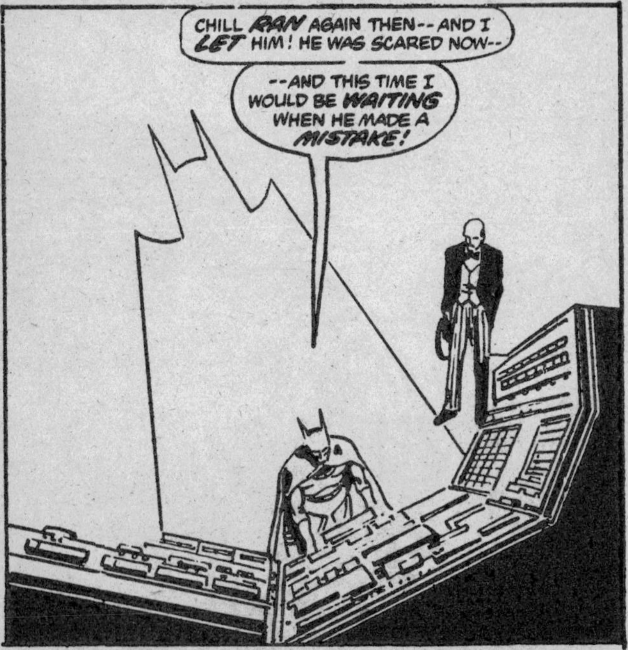
CHILL RAN AGAIN THEN--AND I LET HIM! HE WAS SCARED NOW--
--AND THIS TIME I WOULD BE WAITING WHEN HE MADE A MISTAKE!

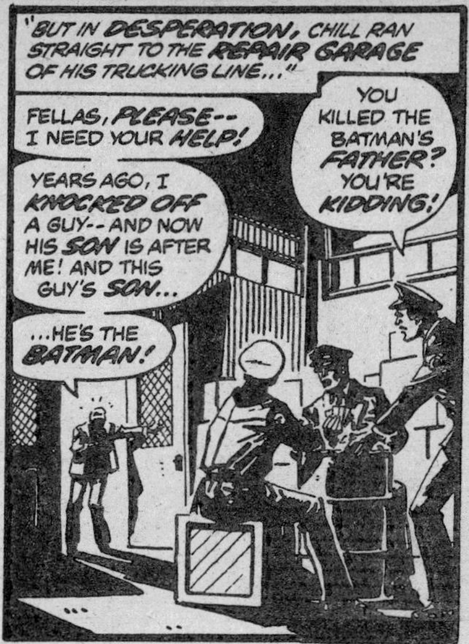
"BUT IN DESPERATION, CHILL RAN STRAIGHT TO THE REPAIR GARAGE OF HIS TRUCKING LINE..."
FELLAS, PLEASE-- I NEED YOUR HELP!
YEARS AGO, I KNOCKED OFF A GUY-- AND NOW HIS SON IS AFTER ME! AND THIS GUY'S SON...
...HE'S THE BATMAN!
YOU KILLED THE BATMAN'S FATHER? YOU'RE KIDDING!

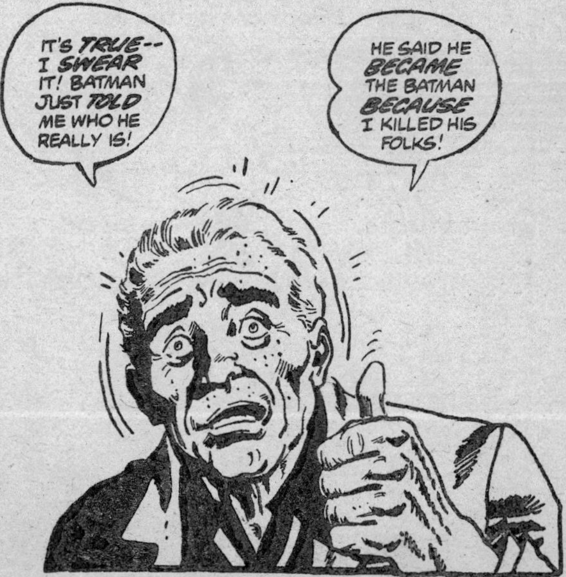
IT'S TRUE-- I SWEAR IT! BATMAN JUST TOLD ME WHO HE REALLY IS!
HE SAID HE BECAME THE BATMAN BECAUSE I KILLED HIS FOLKS!

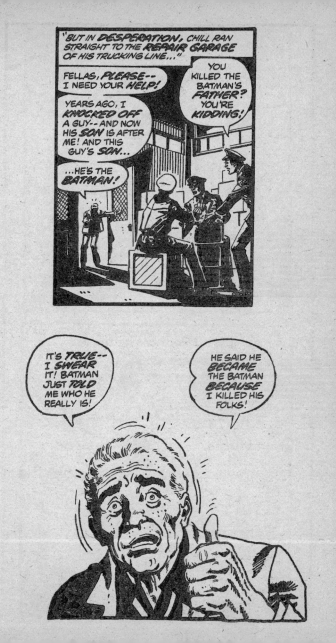

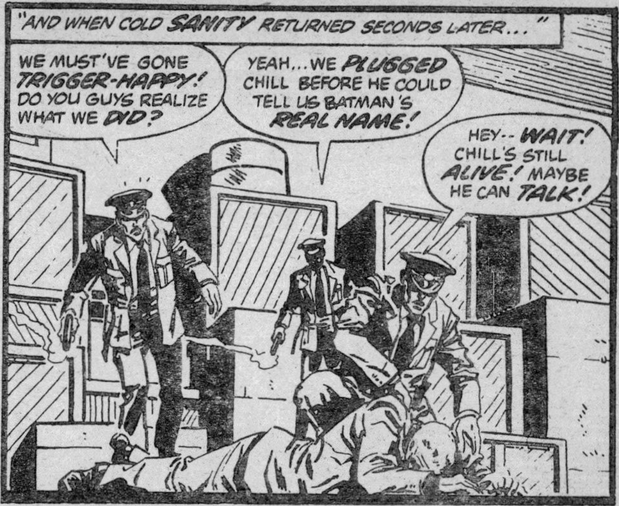
"AND WHEN COLD SANITY RETURNED SECONDS LATER..."
WE MUST'VE GONE TRIGGER-HAPPY! DO YOU GUYS REALIZE WHAT WE DID?
YEAH...WE PLUGGED CHILL BEFORE HE COULD TELL US BATMAN'S REAL NAME!
HEY-- WAIT! CHILL'S STILL ALIVE! MAYBE HE CAN TALK!

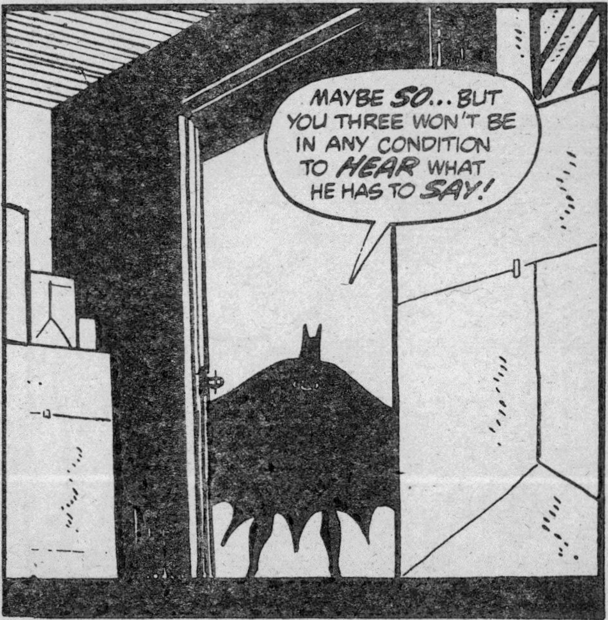
MAYBE SO... BUT YOU THREE WON'T BE IN ANY CONDITION TO HEAR WHAT HE HAS TO SAY!

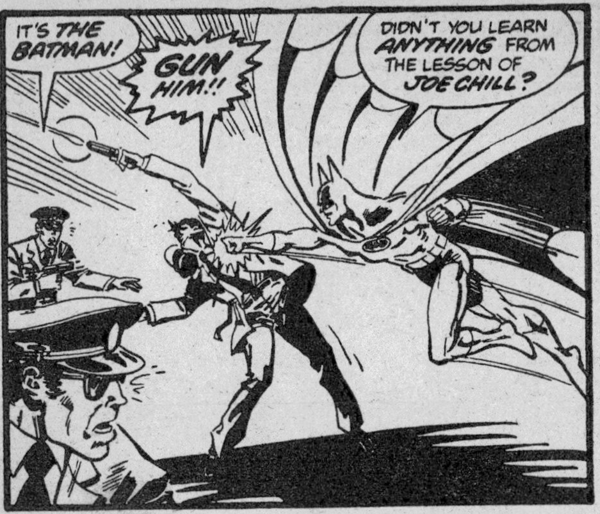
IT'S THE BATMAN!
GUN HIM!!
DIDN'T YOU LEARN ANYTHING FROM THE LESSON OF JOE CHILL?

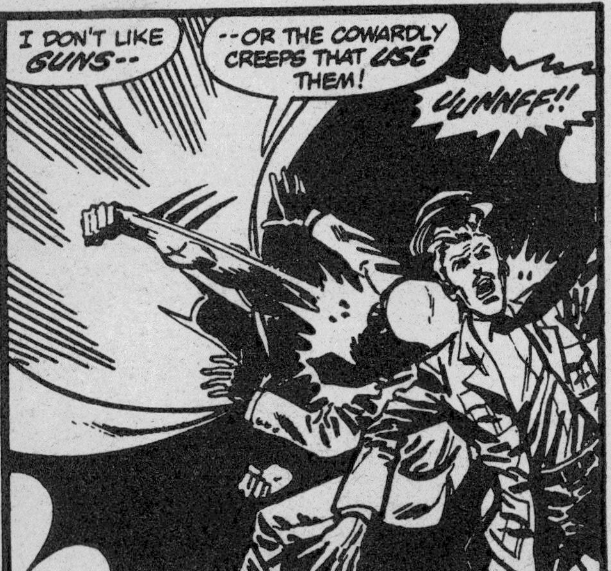
I DON'T LIKE GUNS--
--OR THE COWARDLY CREEPS THAT USE THEM!
UUNNFF!!

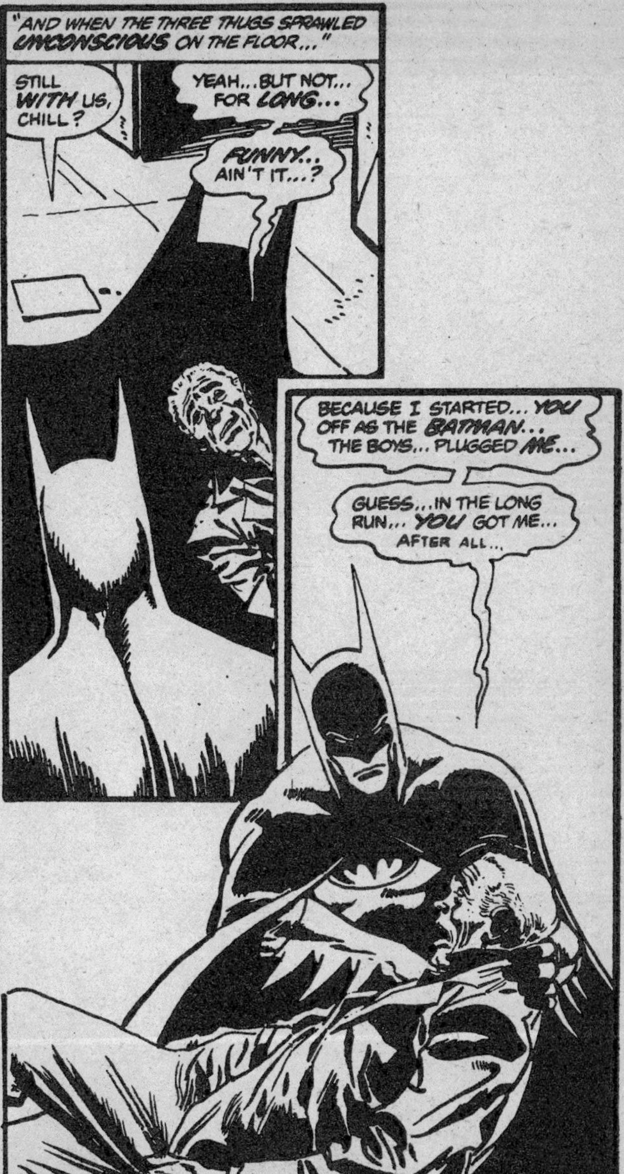
"AND WHEN THE THREE THUGS SPRAWLED UNCONSCIOUS ON THE FLOOR..."
STILL WITH US, CHILL?
YEAH...BUT NOT... FOR LONG...
FUNNY... AIN'T IT...?
BECAUSE I STARTED... YOU OFF AS THE BATMAN... THE BOYS... PLUGGED ME...
GUESS... IN THE LONG RUN... YOU GOT ME... AFTER ALL...

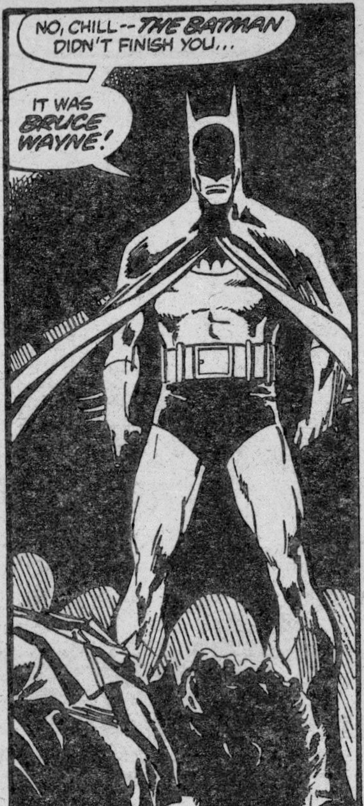
NO, CHILL--THE BATMAN DIDN'T FINISH YOU...
IT WAS BRUCE WAYNE!

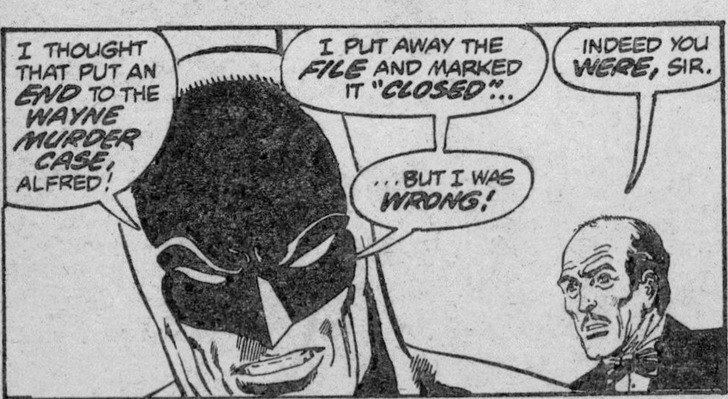
I THOUGHT THAT PUT AN END TO THE WAYNE MURDER CASE, ALFRED!
I PUT AWAY THE FILE AND MARKED IT "CLOSED"...
...BUT I WAS WRONG!
INDEED YOU WERE, SIR.

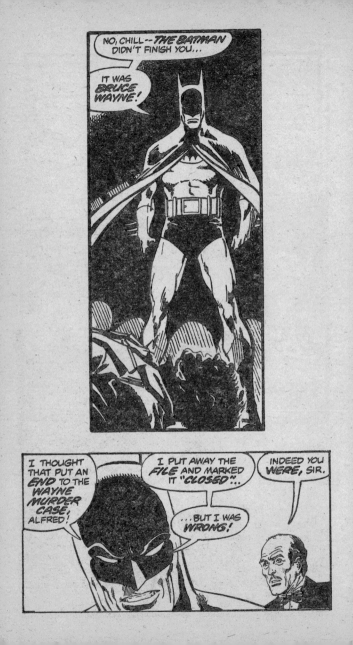

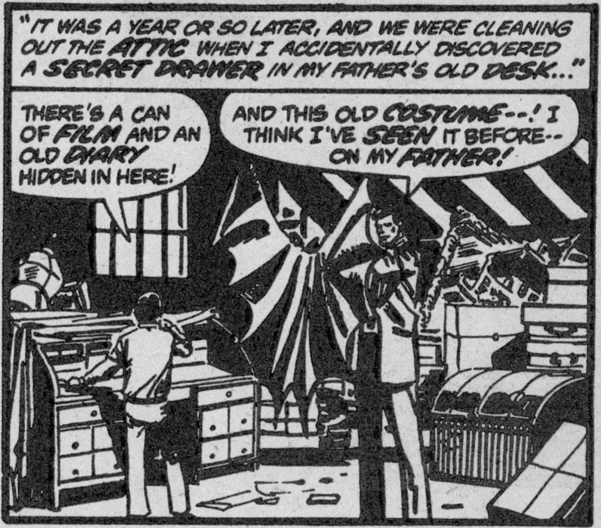
"IT WAS A YEAR OR SO LATER, AND WE WERE CLEANING OUT THE ATTIC WHEN I ACCIDENTALLY DISCOVERED A SECRET DRAWER IN MY FATHER'S OLD DESK..."
THERE'S A CAN OF FILM AND AN OLD DIARY HIDDEN IN HERE!
AND THIS OLD COSTUME--! I THINK I'VE SEEN IT BEFORE-- ON MY FATHER!

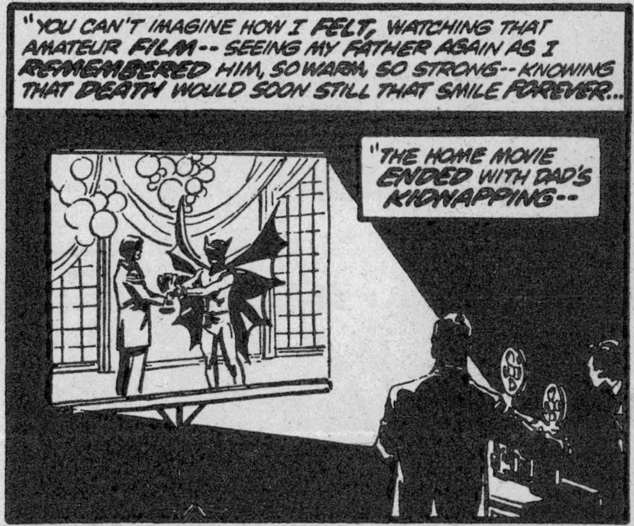
"YOU CAN'T IMAGINE HOW I FELT, WATCHING THAT AMATEUR FILM-- SEEING MY FATHER AGAIN AS I REMEMBERED HIM, SO WARM, SO STRONG--KNOWING THAT DEATH WOULD SOON STILL THAT SMILE FOREVER...
"THE HOME MOVIE ENDED WITH DAD'S KIDNAPPING--

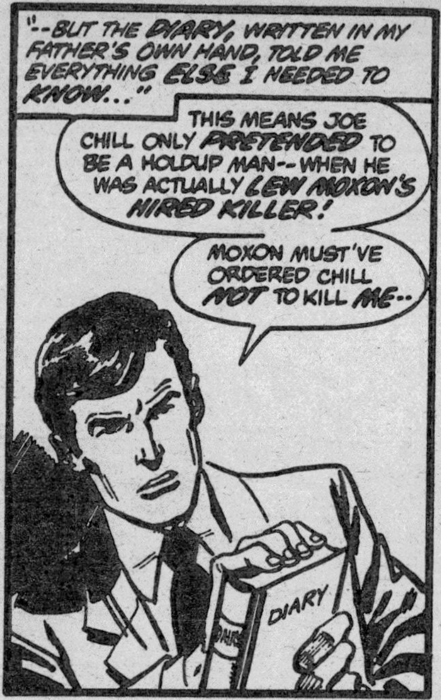
"--BUT THE DIARY, WRITTEN IN MY FATHER'S OWN HAND, TOLD ME EVERYTHING ELSE I NEEDED TO KNOW..."
THIS MEANS JOE CHILL ONLY PRETENDED TO BE A HOLDUP MAN--WHEN HE WAS ACTUALLY LEW MOXON'S HIRED KILLER!
MOXON MUST'VE ORDERED CHILL NOT TO KILL ME--
DIARY

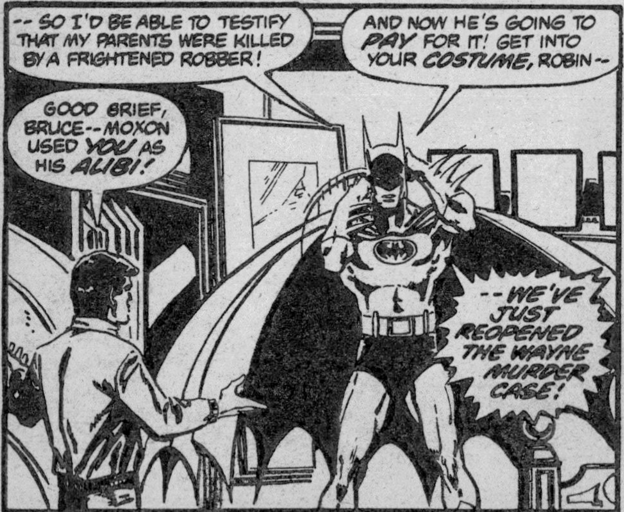
-- SO I'D BE ABLE TO TESTIFY THAT MY PARENTS WERE KILLED BY A FRIGHTENED ROBBER!
GOOD GRIEF, BRUCE--MOXON USED YOU AS HIS ALIBI!
AND NOW HE'S GOING TO PAY FOR IT! GET INTO YOUR COSTUME, ROBIN--
--WE'VE JUST REOPENED THE WAYNE MURDER CASE!

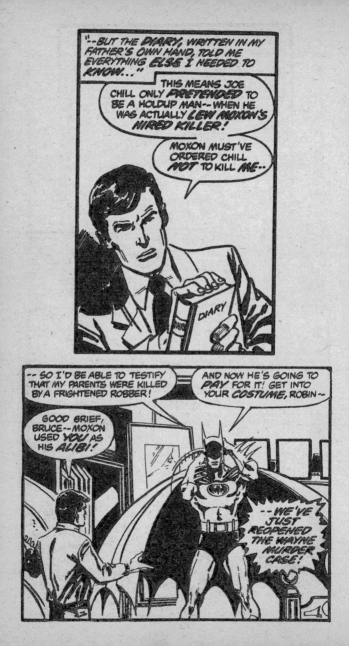

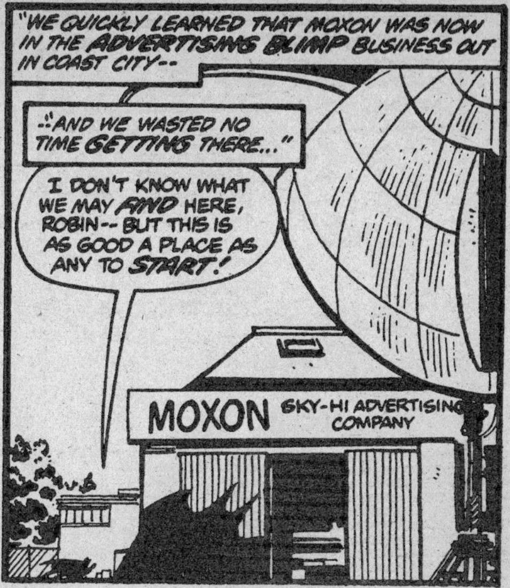
"WE QUICKLY LEARNED THAT MOXON WAS NOW IN THE ADVERTISING BLIMP BUSINESS OUT IN COAST CITY--
--"AND WE WASTED NO TIME GETTING THERE..."
I DON'T KNOW WHAT WE MAY FIND HERE, ROBIN-- BUT THIS IS AS GOOD A PLACE AS ANY TO START!
MOXON SKY-HI ADVERTISING COMPANY

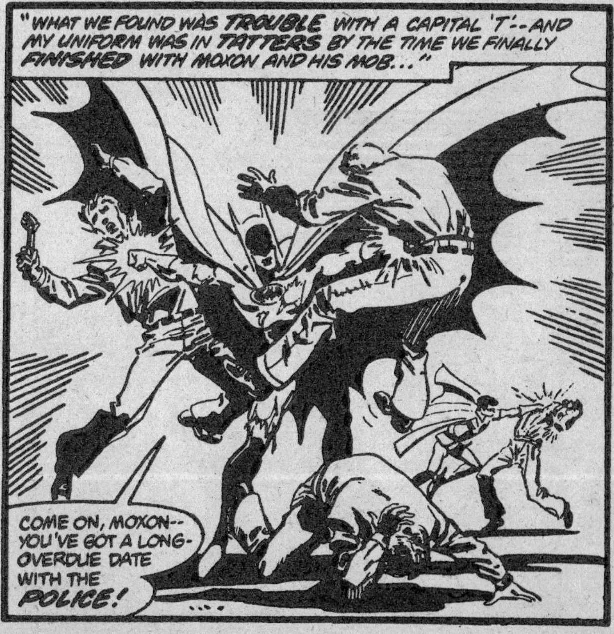
"WHAT WE FOUND WAS TROUBLE WITH A CAPITAL 'T'--AND MY UNIFORM WAS IN TATTERS BY THE TIME WE FINALLY FINISHED WITH MOXON AND HIS MOB..."
COME ON, MOXON-- YOU'VE GOT A LONG-OVERDUE DATE WITH THE POLICE!
...

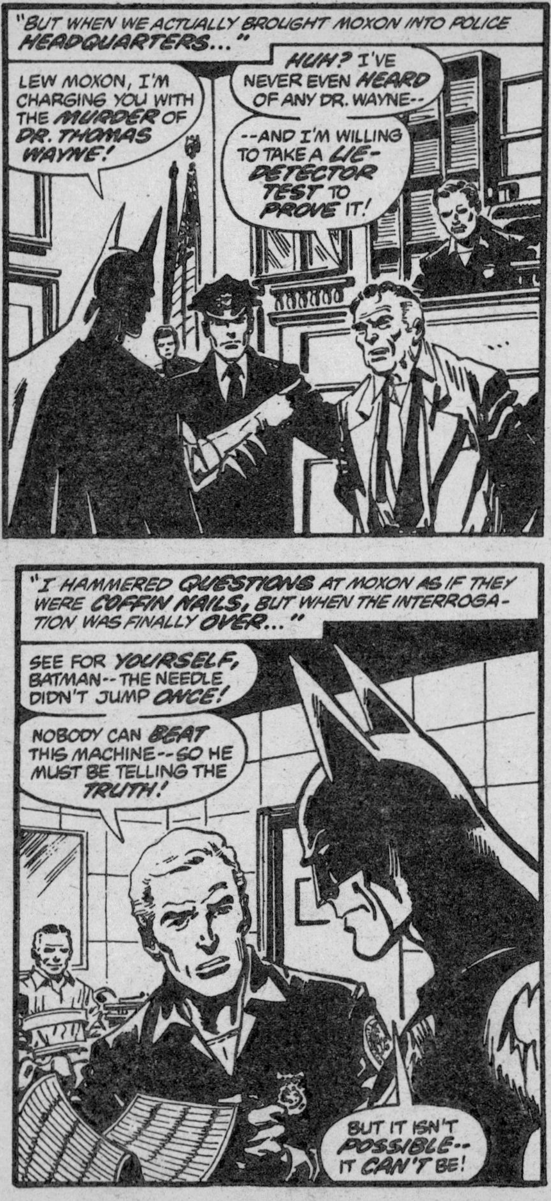
"BUT WHEN WE ACTUALLY BROUGHT MOXON INTO POLICE HEADQUARTERS..."
LEW MOXON, I'M CHARGING YOU WITH THE MURDER OF DR. THOMAS WAYNE!
HUH? I'VE NEVER EVEN HEARD OF ANY DR. WAYNE--
--AND I'M WILLING TO TAKE A LIE-DETECTOR TEST TO PROVE IT!
"I HAMMERED QUESTIONS AT MOXON AS IF THEY WERE COFFIN NAILS, BUT WHEN THE INTERROGATION WAS FINALLY OVER..."
SEE FOR YOURSELF, BATMAN--THE NEEDLE DIDN'T JUMP ONCE!
NOBODY CAN BEAT THIS MACHINE--SO HE MUST BE TELLING THE TRUTH!
BUT IT ISN'T POSSIBLE.. IT CAN'T BE!

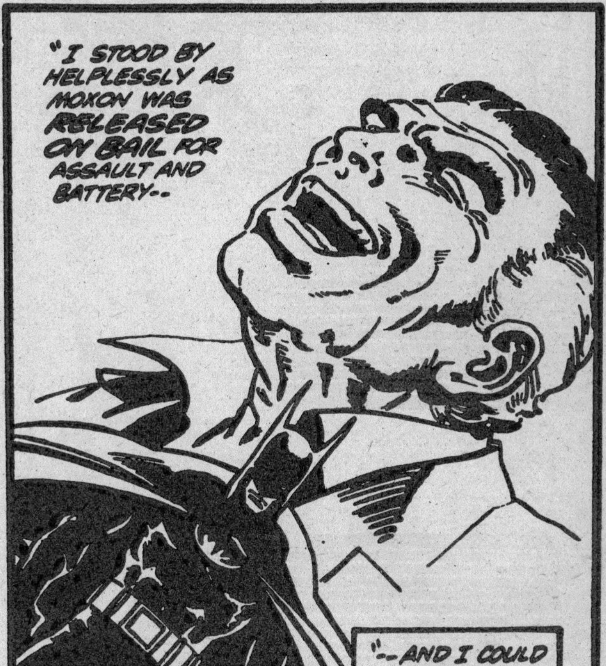
"I STOOD BY HELPLESSLY AS MOXON WAS RELEASED ON BAIL FOR ASSAULT AND BATTERY--
"--AND I COULD FEEL HIM LAUGHING AT ME BEHIND MY BACK ALL THE WAY!

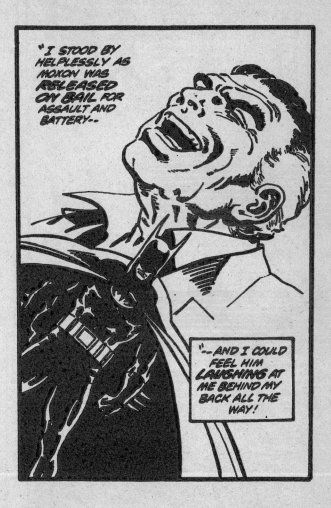

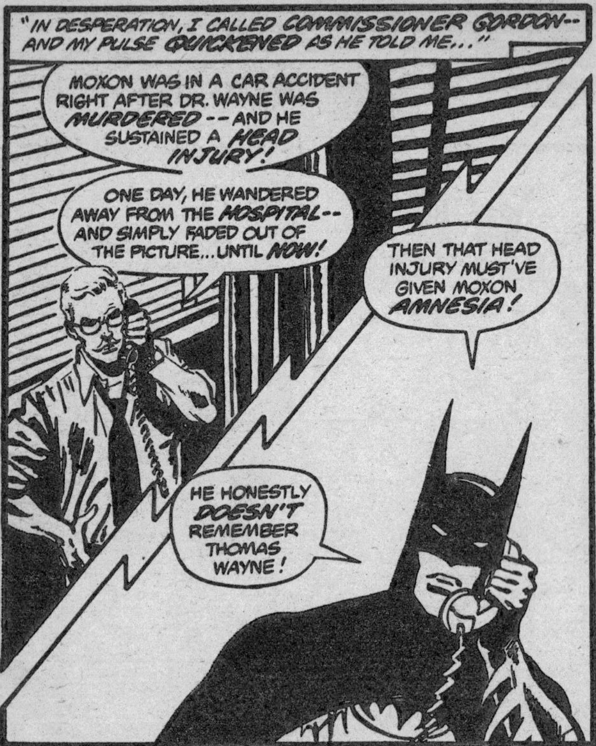
"IN DESPERATION, I CALLED COMMISSIONER GORDON-- AND MY PULSE QUICKENED AS HE TOLD ME..."
MOXON WAS IN A CAR ACCIDENT RIGHT AFTER DR. WAYNE WAS MURDERED -- AND HE SUSTAINED A HEAD INJURY!
ONE DAY, HE WANDERED AWAY FROM THE HOSPITAL-- AND SIMPLY FADED OUT OF THE PICTURE...UNTIL NOW!
THEN THAT HEAD INJURY MUST'VE GIVEN MOXON AMNESIA!
HE HONESTLY DOESN'T REMEMBER THOMAS WAYNE!

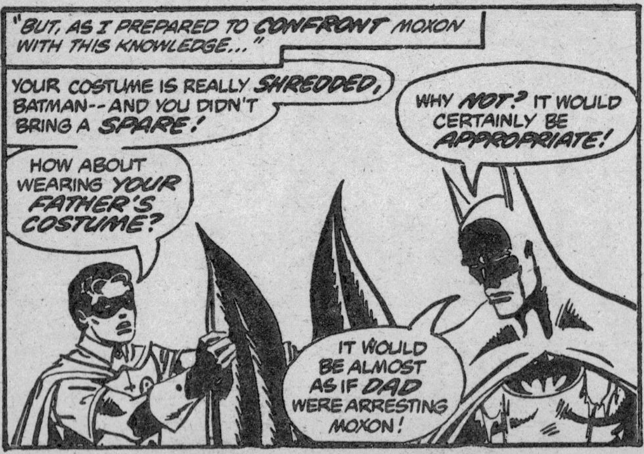
"BUT, AS I PREPARED TO CONFRONT MOXON WITH THIS KNOWLEDGE..."
YOUR COSTUME IS REALLY SHREDDED, BATMAN--AND YOU DIDN'T BRING A SPARE!
HOW ABOUT WEARING YOUR FATHER'S COSTUME?
WHY NOT? IT WOULD CERTAINLY BE APPROPRIATE!
IT WOULD BE ALMOST AS IF DAD WERE ARRESTING MOXON!

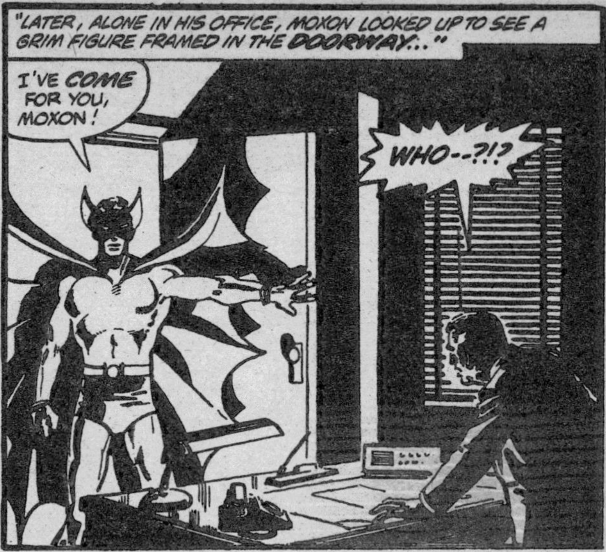
"LATER, ALONE IN HIS OFFICE, MOXON LOOKED UP TO SEE A GRIM FIGURE FRAMED IN THE DOORWAY..."
I'VE COME FOR YOU, MOXON!
WHO--?!?

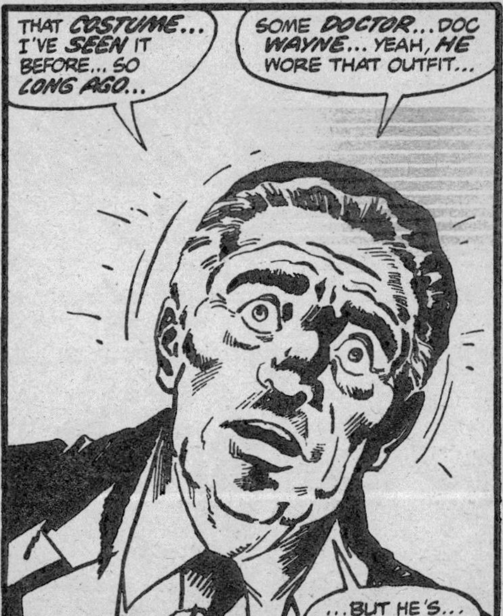
THAT COSTUME... I'VE SEEN IT BEFORE... SO LONG AGO...
SOME DOCTOR... DOC WAYNE... YEAH, HE WORE THAT OUTFIT...
...BUT HE'S... HE'S DEAD...

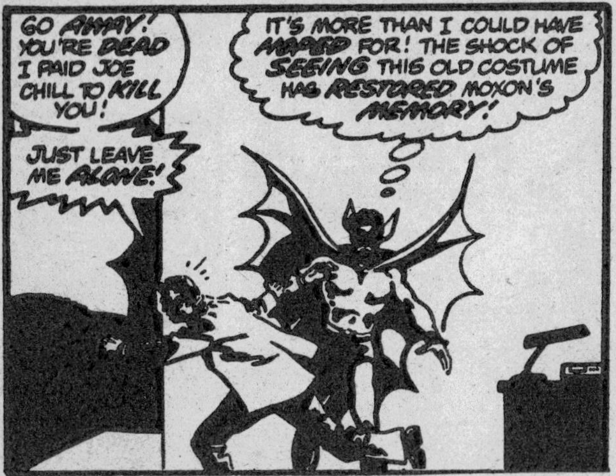
GO AWAY! YOU'RE DEAD I PAID JOE CHILL TO KILL YOU!
IT'S MORE THAN I COULD HAVE HOPED FOR! THE SHOCK OF SEEING THIS OLD COSTUME HAS RESTORED MOXON'S MEMORY!
JUST LEAVE ME ALONE!

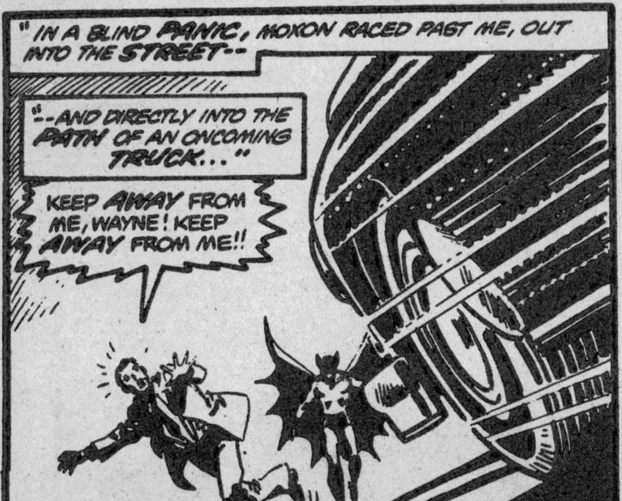
"IN A BLIND PANIC, MOXON RACED PAST ME, OUT INTO THE STREET--
"--AND DIRECTLY INTO THE PATH OF AN ONCOMING TRUCK..."
KEEP AWAY FROM ME, WAYNE! KEEP AWAY FROM ME!!

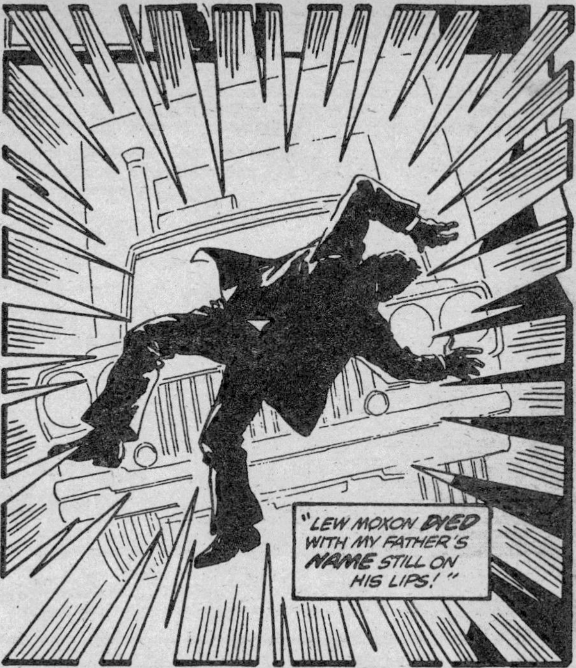
"LEW MOXON DYED WITH MY FATHER'S NAME STILL ON HIS LIPS!"

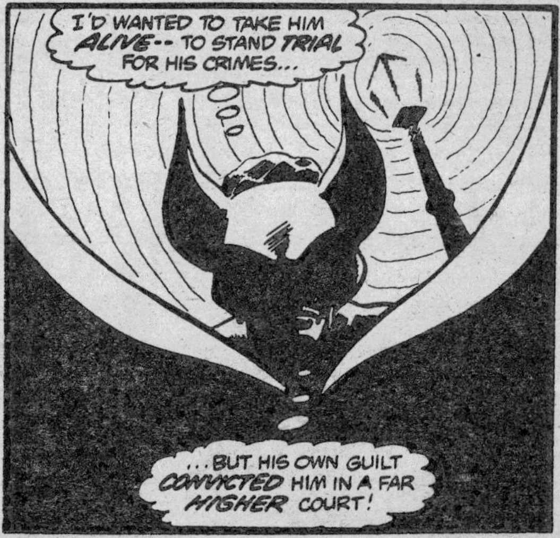
I'D WANTED TO TAKE HIM ALIVE-- TO STAND TRIAL FOR HIS CRIMES...
...BUT HIS OWN GUILT CONVICTED HIM IN A FAR HIGHER COURT!

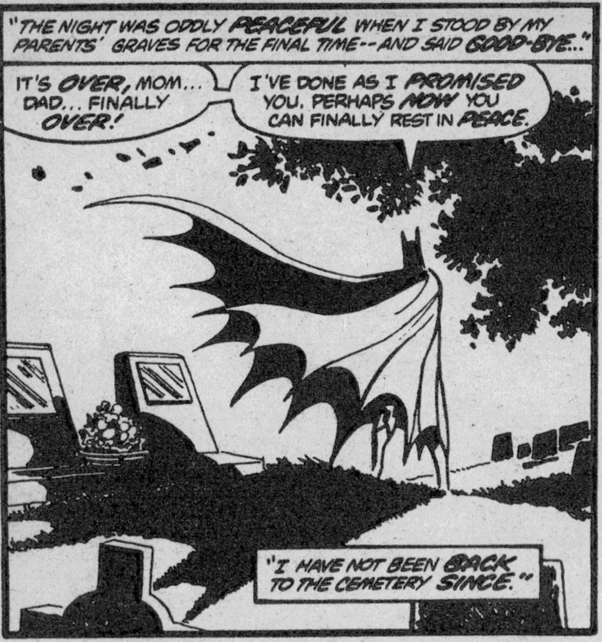
"THE NIGHT WAS ODDLY PEACEFUL WHEN I STOOD BY MY PARENTS' GRAVES FOR THE FINAL TIME--AND SAID GOOD-BYE..."
IT'S OVER, MOM... DAD... FINALLY OVER!
I'VE DONE AS I PROMISED YOU. PERHAPS NOW YOU CAN FINALLY REST IN PEACE.
"I HAVE NOT BEEN BACK TO THE CEMETERY SINCE."

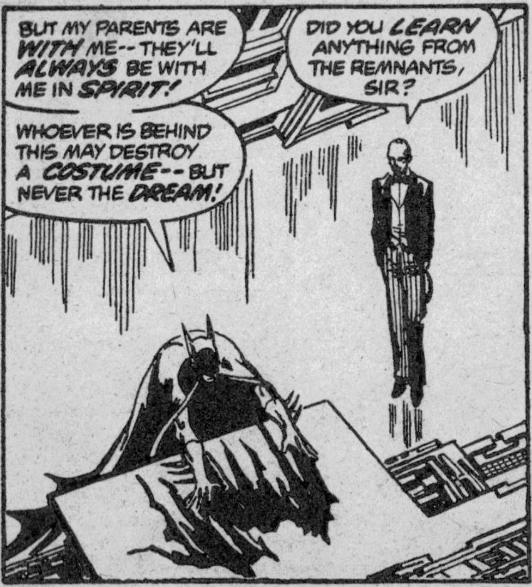
BUT MY PARENTS ARE WITH ME--THEY'LL ALWAYS BE WITH ME IN SPIRIT!
DID YOU LEARN ANYTHING FROM THE REMNANTS, SIR?
WHOEVER IS BEHIND THIS MAY DESTROY A COSTUME--BUT NEVER THE DREAM!

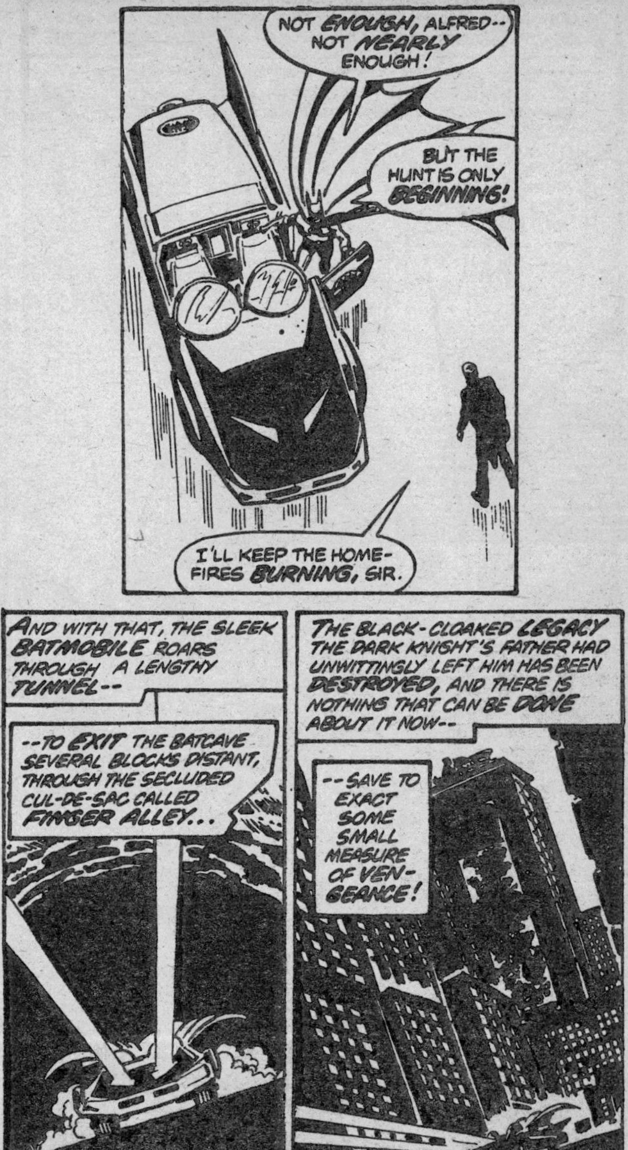
NOT ENOUGH, ALFRED-- NOT NEARLY ENOUGH!
BUT THE HUNT IS ONLY BEGINNING!
I'LL KEEP THE HOME-FIRES BURNING, SIR.
AND WITH THAT, THE SLEEK BATMOBILE ROARS THROUGH A LENGTHY TUNNEL--
--TO EXIT THE BATCAVE SEVERAL BLOCKS DISTANT, THROUGH THE SECLUDED CUL-DE-SAC CALLED FINGER ALLEY...
THE BLACK-CLOAKED LEGACY THE DARK KNIGHT'S FATHER HAD UNWITTINGLY LEFT HIM HAS BEEN DESTROYED, AND THERE IS NOTHING THAT CAN BE DONE ABOUT IT NOW--
--SAVE TO EXACT SOME SMALL MEASURE OF VEN-GEANCE!

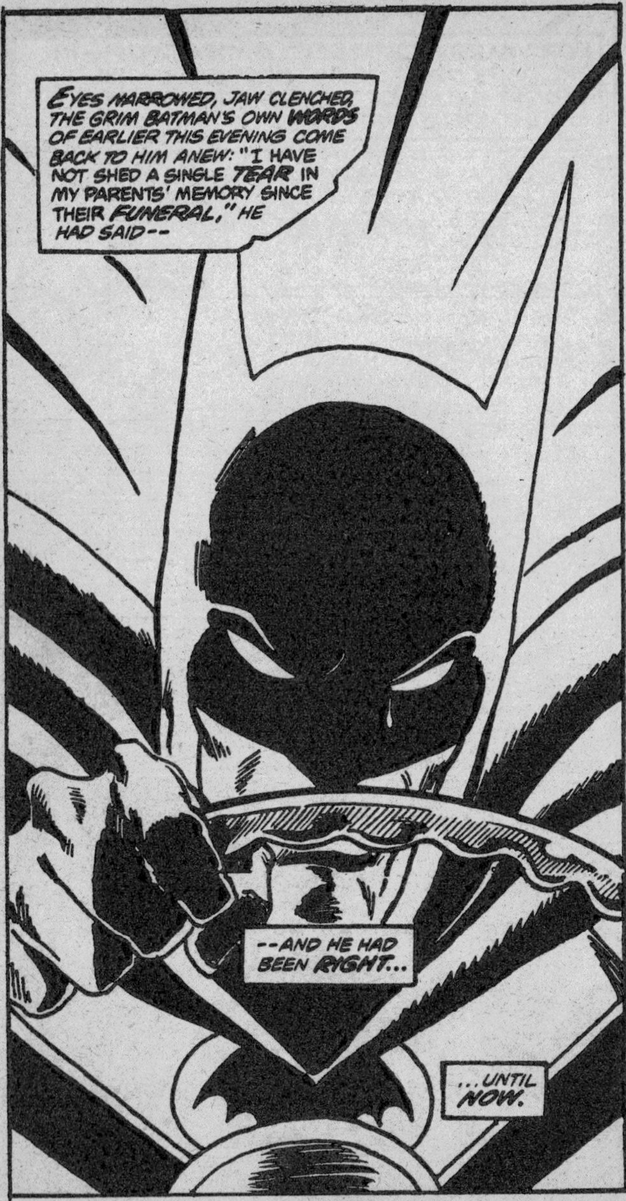
EYES NARROWED, JAW CLENCHED, THE GRIM BATMAN'S OWN WORDS OF EARLIER THIS EVENING COME BACK TO HIM ANEW: "I HAVE NOT SHED A SINGLE TEAR IN MY PARENTS' MEMORY SINCE THEIR FUNERAL," HE HAD SAID--
--AND HE HAD BEEN RIGHT...
...UNTIL NOW.

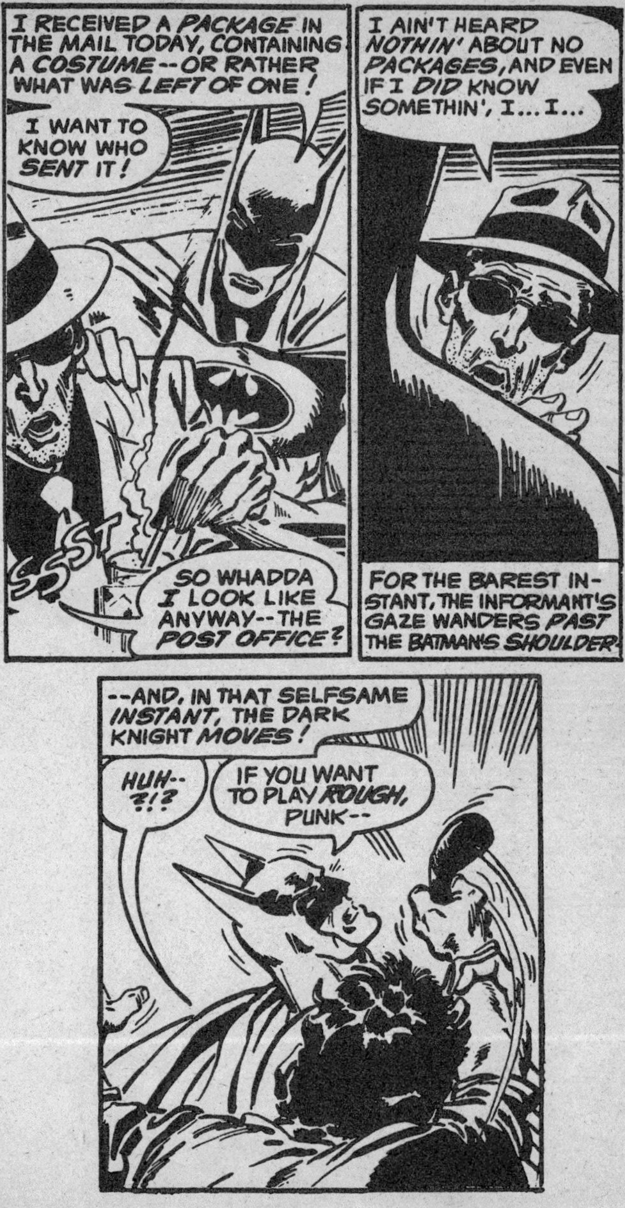
I RECEIVED A PACKAGE IN THE MAIL TODAY, CONTAINING A COSTUME--OR RATHER WHAT WAS LEFT OF ONE!
I WANT TO KNOW WHO SENT IT!
SSSST
SO WHADDA I LOOK LIKE ANYWAY--THE POST OFFICE?
I AIN'T HEARD NOTHIN' ABOUT NO PACKAGES, AND EVEN IF I DID KNOW SOMETHIN', I... I...
FOR THE BAREST INSTANT, THE INFORMANT'S GAZE WANDERS PAST THE BATMAN'S SHOULDER-
--AND, IN THAT SELFSAME INSTANT, THE DARK KNIGHT MOVES!
HUH--?!?
IF YOU WANT TO PLAY ROUGH, PUNK--

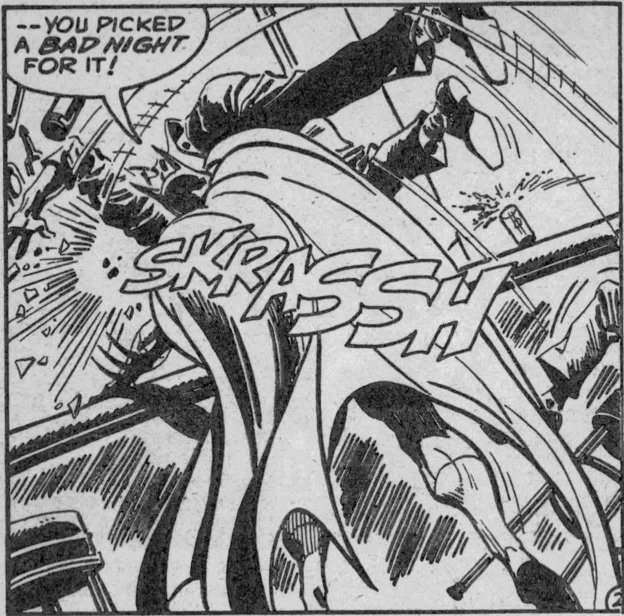
--YOU PICKED A BAD NIGHT FOR IT!
SMRASSH
2

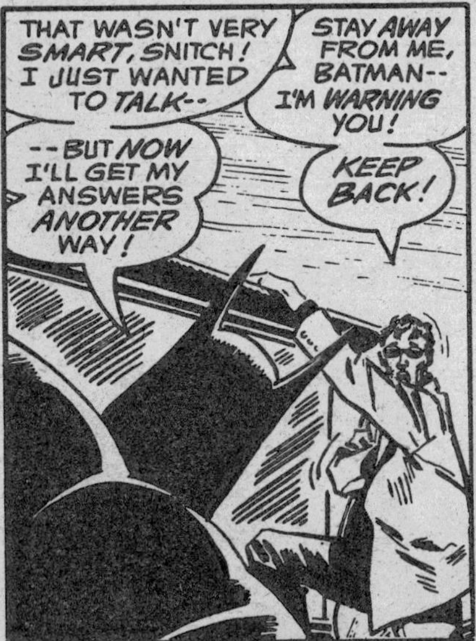
THAT WASN'T VERY SMART, SNITCH! I JUST WANTED TO TALK--
STAY AWAY FROM ME, BATMAN-- I'M WARNING YOU!
--BUT NOW I'LL GET MY ANSWERS ANOTHER WAY!
KEEP BACK!

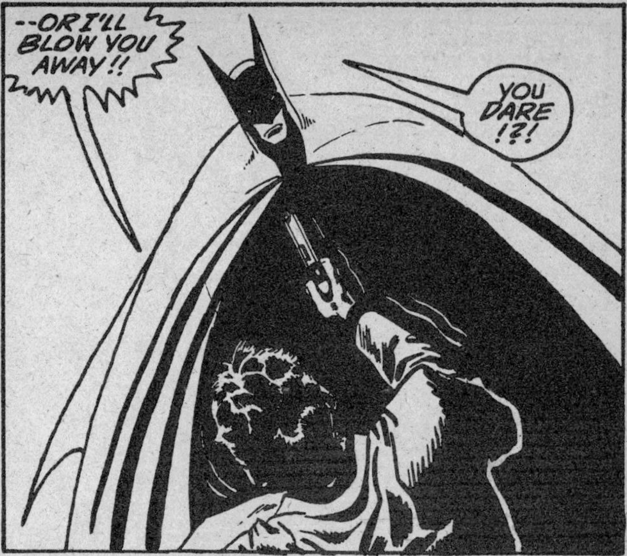
--OR I'LL BLOW YOU AWAY!!
YOU DARE !?!

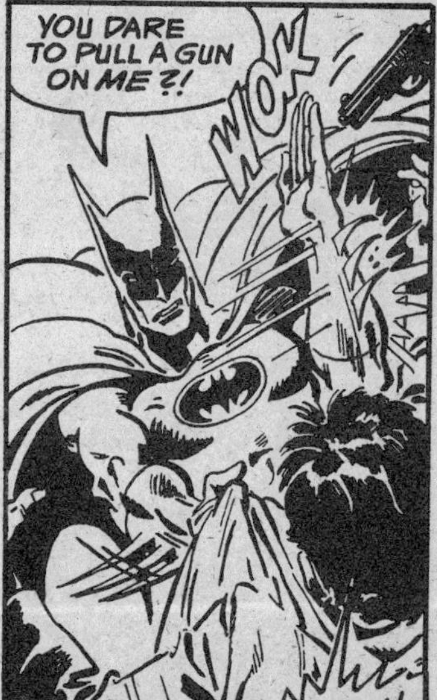
YOU DARE TO PULL A GUN ON ME?!
WOK
HHUUNH!

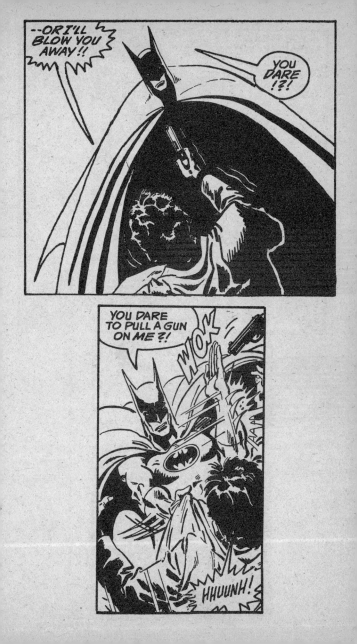

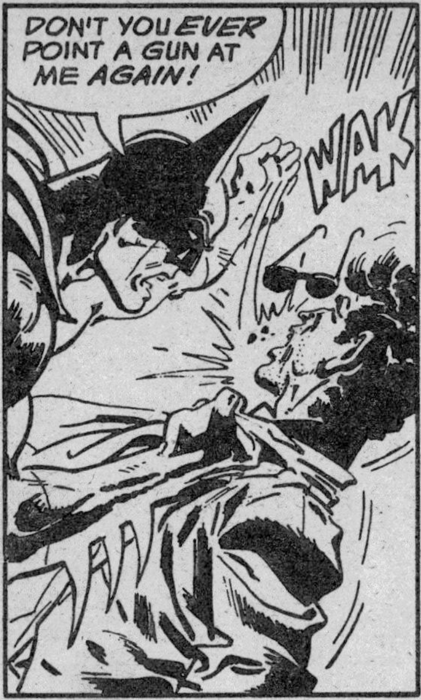
DON'T YOU EVER POINT A GUN AT ME AGAIN!
WAK

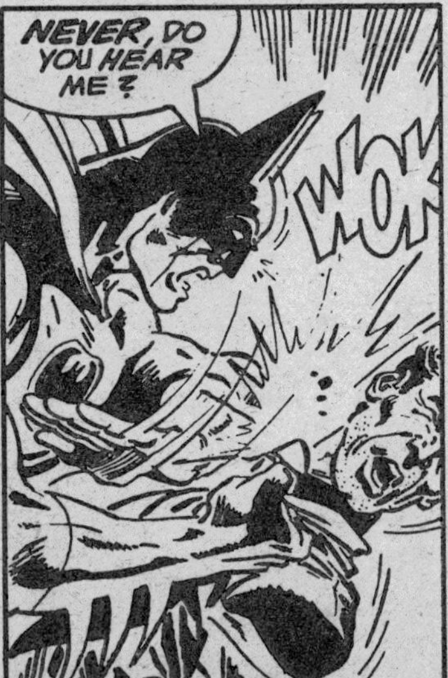
NEVER, DO YOU HEAR ME?
WOK

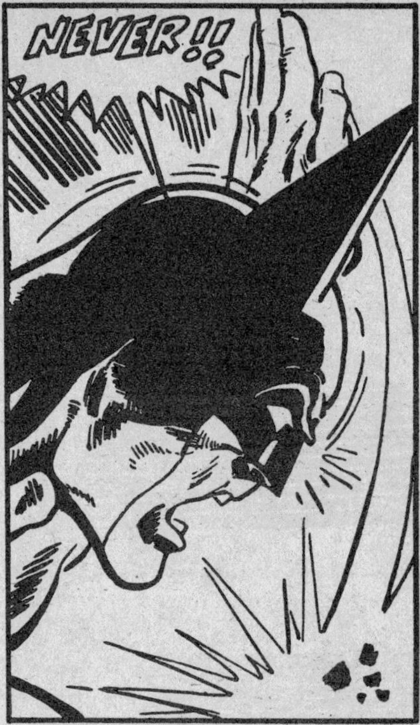
NEVER!!

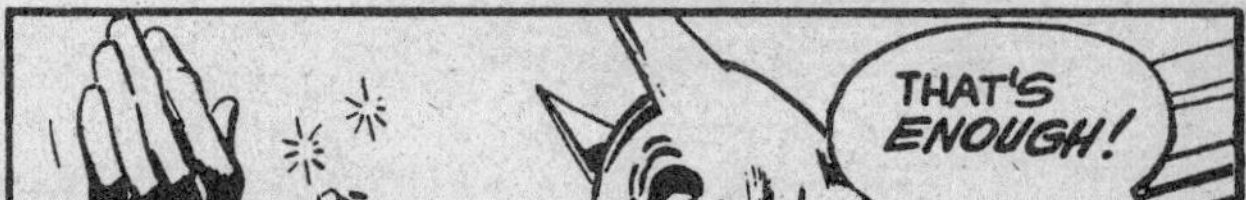
THAT'S ENOUGH!
EH?

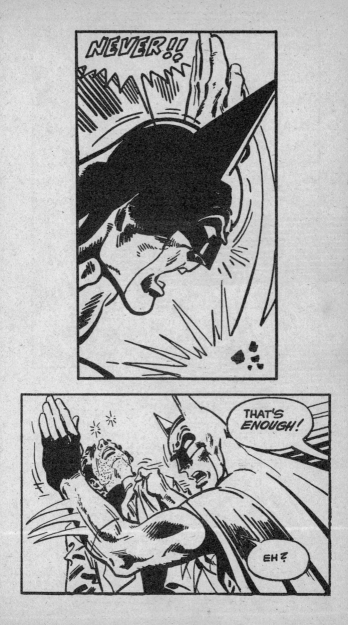

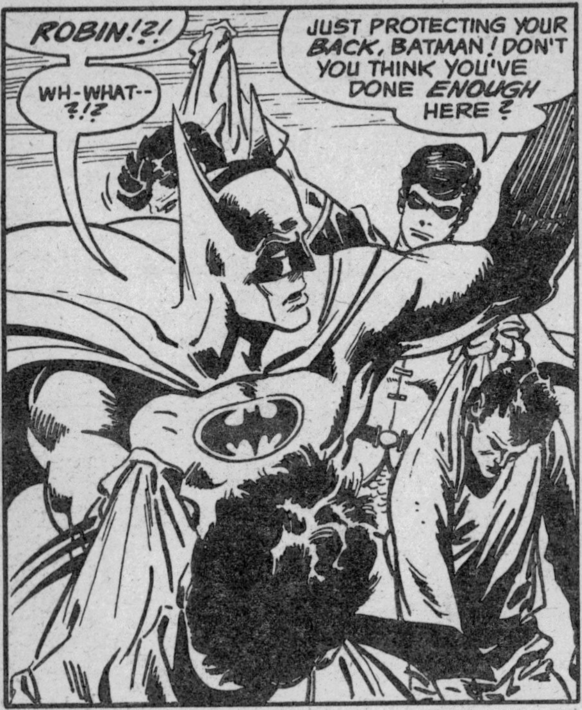
ROBIN!?!
WH-WHAT-- ?!?
JUST PROTECTING YOUR BACK, BATMAN! DON'T YOU THINK YOU'VE DONE ENOUGH HERE?

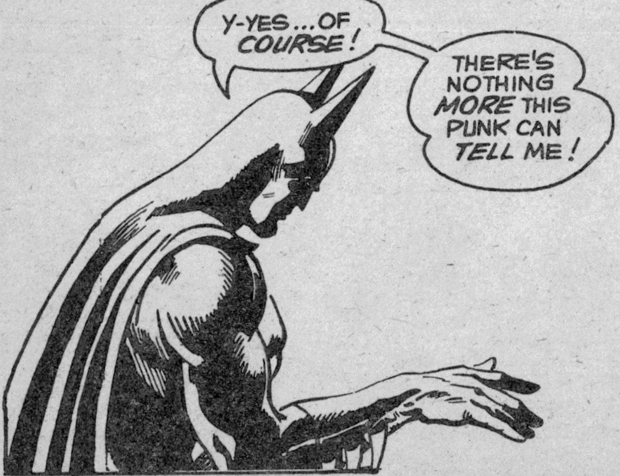
Y-YES...OF COURSE!
THERE'S NOTHING MORE THIS PUNK CAN TELL ME!

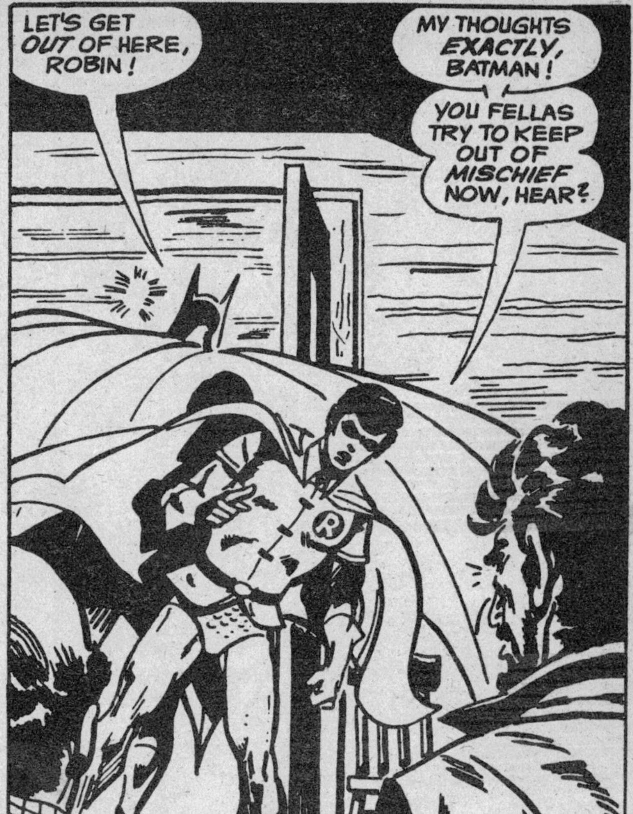
LET'S GET *OUT* OF HERE, ROBIN!
MY THOUGHTS *EXACTLY,* BATMAN!
YOU FELLAS TRY TO KEEP OUT OF *MISCHIEF* NOW, HEAR?
THE FACES THAT WATCH THE *CAPED CRUSADERS* AS THEY *LEAVE* THE BATTLE-TORN ROOM ARE FLUSHED WITH AN AWKWARD MIXTURE OF *HATRED*-- AND *RELIEF*...

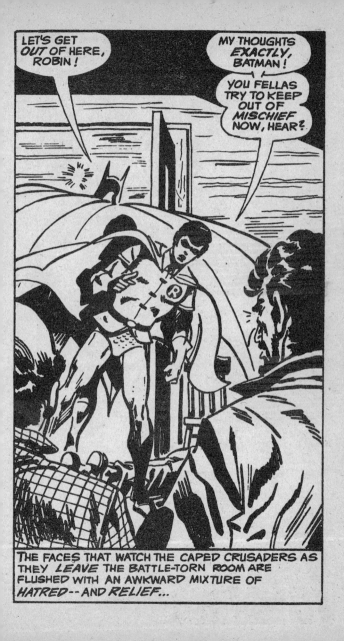

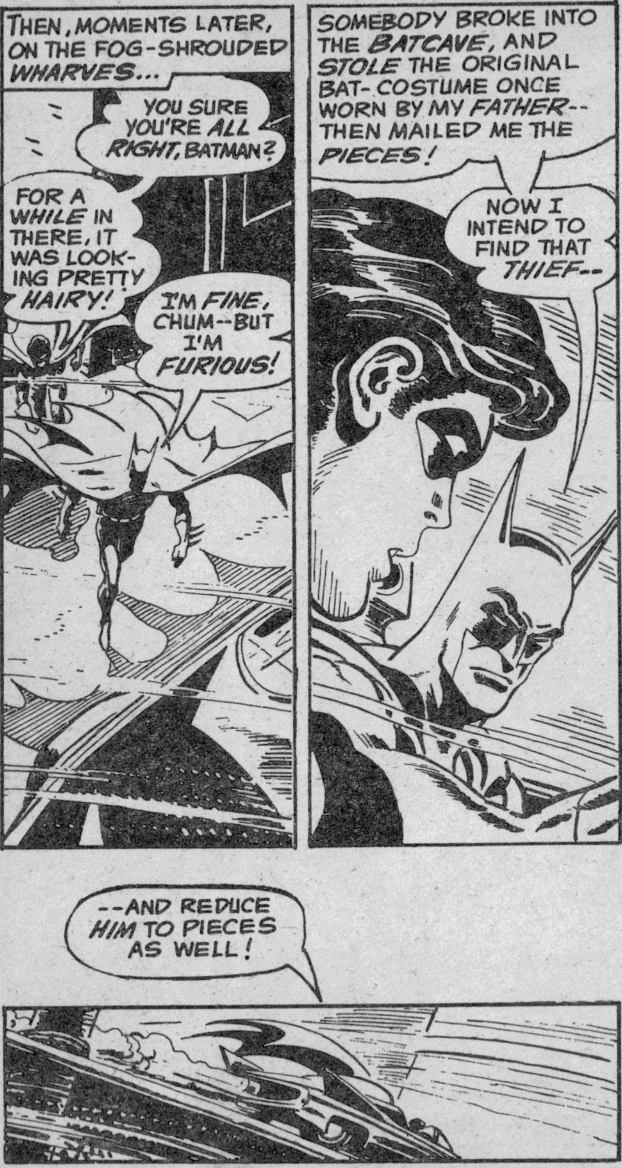
THEN, MOMENTS LATER, ON THE FOG-SHROUDED WHARVES...
YOU SURE YOU'RE ALL RIGHT, BATMAN?
FOR A WHILE IN THERE, IT WAS LOOKING PRETTY HAIRY!
I'M FINE, CHUM--BUT I'M FURIOUS!
SOMEBODY BROKE INTO THE BATCAVE, AND STOLE THE ORIGINAL BAT-COSTUME ONCE WORN BY MY FATHER--THEN MAILED ME THE PIECES!
NOW I INTEND TO FIND THAT THIEF--
--AND REDUCE HIM TO PIECES AS WELL!

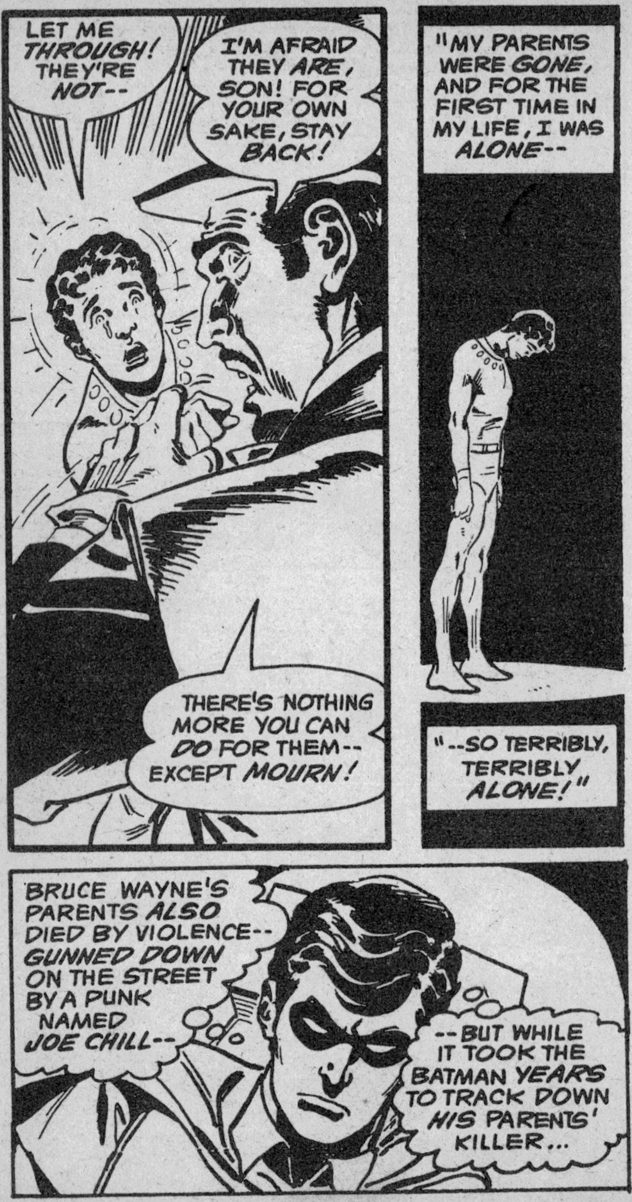

LET ME THROUGH! THEY'RE NOT--
I'M AFRAID THEY ARE, SON! FOR YOUR OWN SAKE, STAY BACK!
THERE'S NOTHING MORE YOU CAN DO FOR THEM--EXCEPT MOURN!
"MY PARENTS WERE GONE, AND FOR THE FIRST TIME IN MY LIFE, I WAS ALONE--
"--SO TERRIBLY, TERRIBLY ALONE!"
BRUCE WAYNE'S PARENTS ALSO DIED BY VIOLENCE--GUNNED DOWN ON THE STREET BY A PUNK NAMED JOE CHILL--
--BUT WHILE IT TOOK THE BATMAN YEARS TO TRACK DOWN HIS PARENTS' KILLER...

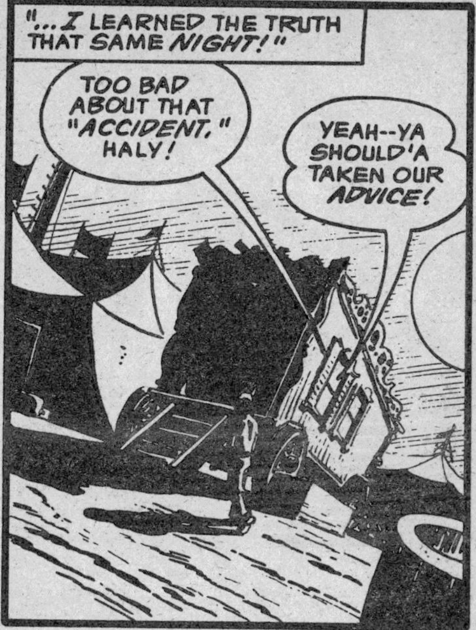
"...I LEARNED THE TRUTH THAT SAME NIGHT!"
TOO BAD ABOUT THAT "ACCIDENT," HALY!
YEAH--YA SHOULD'A TAKEN OUR ADVICE!

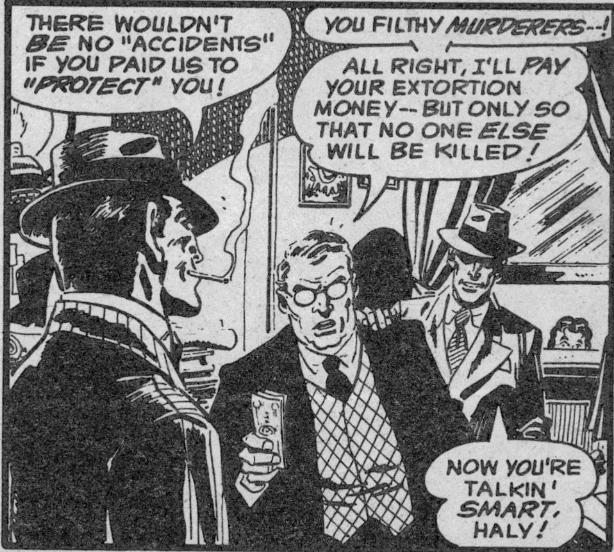
THERE WOULDN'T BE NO "ACCIDENTS" IF YOU PAID US TO "PROTECT" YOU!
YOU FILTHY MURDERERS--!
ALL RIGHT, I'LL PAY YOUR EXTORTION MONEY-- BUT ONLY SO THAT NO ONE ELSE WILL BE KILLED!
NOW YOU'RE TALKIN' SMART, HALY!

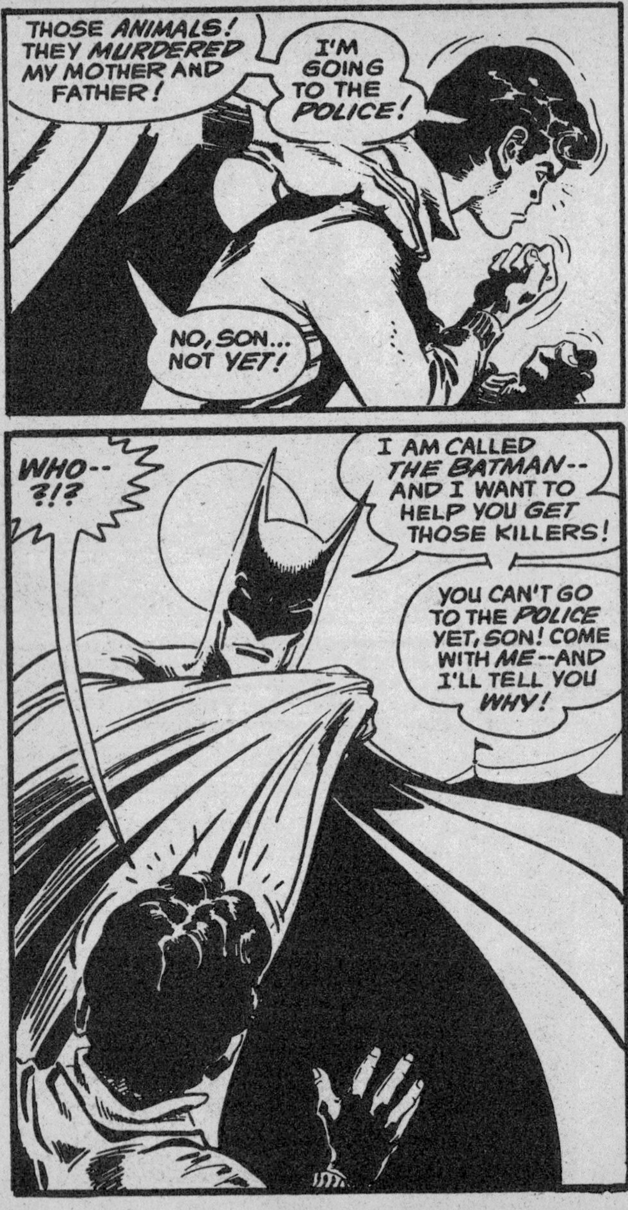
THOSE ANIMALS! THEY MURDERED MY MOTHER AND FATHER!
I'M GOING TO THE POLICE!
NO, SON... NOT YET!
WHO-- ?!?
I AM CALLED THE BATMAN-- AND I WANT TO HELP YOU GET THOSE KILLERS!
YOU CAN'T GO TO THE POLICE YET, SON! COME WITH ME--AND I'LL TELL YOU WHY!

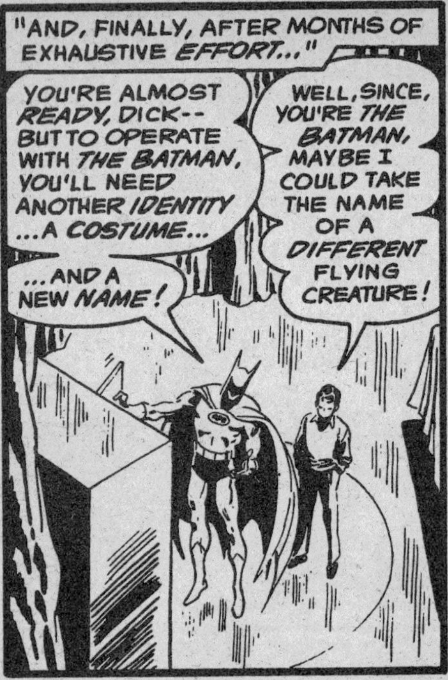
"AND, FINALLY, AFTER MONTHS OF EXHAUSTIVE EFFORT..."
YOU'RE ALMOST READY, DICK-- BUT TO OPERATE WITH THE BATMAN, YOU'LL NEED ANOTHER IDENTITY ...A COSTUME...
...AND A NEW NAME!
WELL, SINCE, YOU'RE THE BATMAN, MAYBE I COULD TAKE THE NAME OF A DIFFERENT FLYING CREATURE!

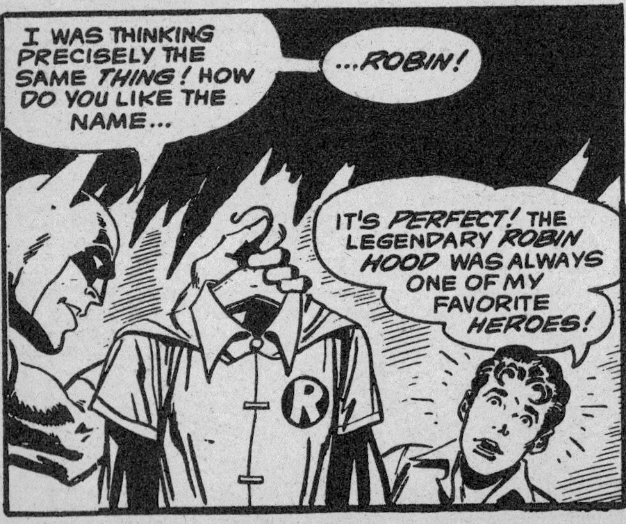
I WAS THINKING PRECISELY THE SAME THING! HOW DO YOU LIKE THE NAME...
...ROBIN!
IT'S PERFECT! THE LEGENDARY ROBIN HOOD WAS ALWAYS ONE OF MY FAVORITE HEROES!

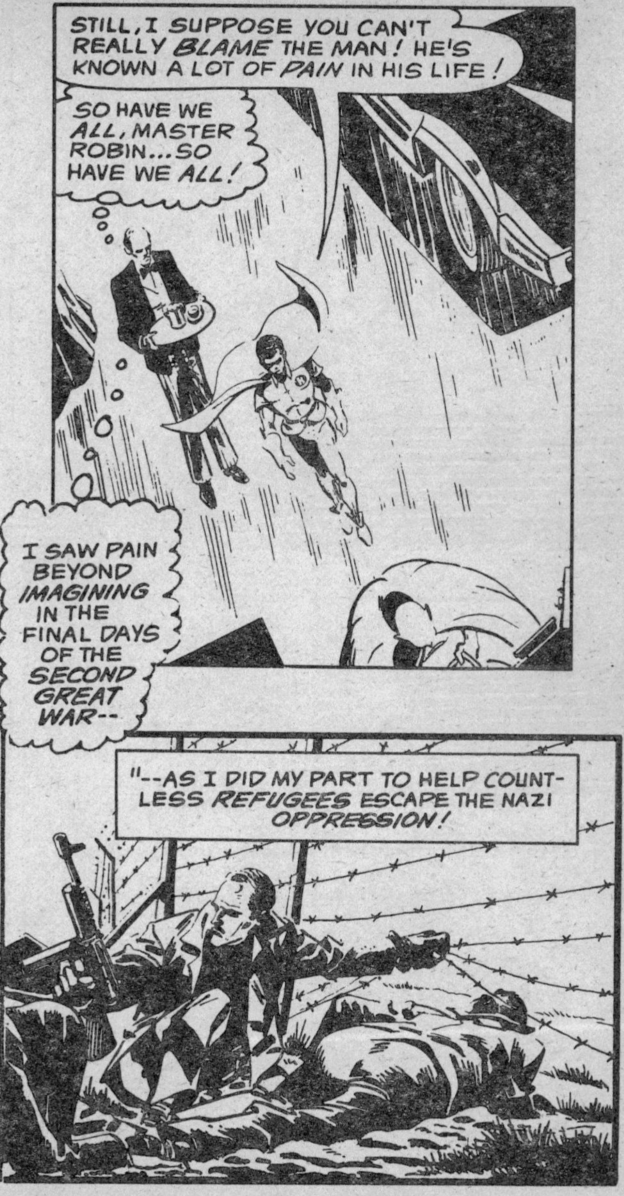
STILL, I SUPPOSE YOU CAN'T REALLY BLAME THE MAN! HE'S KNOWN A LOT OF PAIN IN HIS LIFE!
SO HAVE WE ALL, MASTER ROBIN... SO HAVE WE ALL!
I SAW PAIN BEYOND IMAGINING IN THE FINAL DAYS OF THE SECOND GREAT WAR--
"--AS I DID MY PART TO HELP COUNTLESS REFUGEES ESCAPE THE NAZI OPPRESSION!

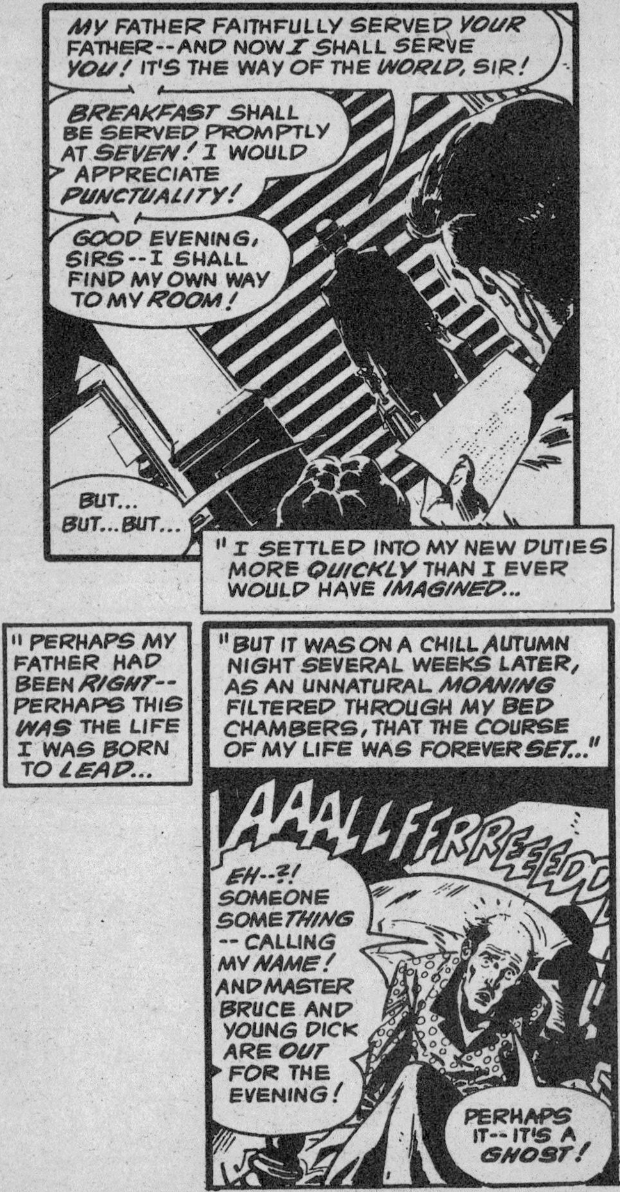

MY FATHER FAITHFULLY SERVED YOUR FATHER--AND NOW I SHALL SERVE YOU! IT'S THE WAY OF THE WORLD, SIR!
BREAKFAST SHALL BE SERVED PROMPTLY AT SEVEN! I WOULD APPRECIATE PUNCTUALITY!
GOOD EVENING, SIRS--I SHALL FIND MY OWN WAY TO MY ROOM!
BUT... BUT...BUT...
"I SETTLED INTO MY NEW DUTIES MORE QUICKLY THAN I EVER WOULD HAVE IMAGINED...
"PERHAPS MY FATHER HAD BEEN RIGHT--PERHAPS THIS WAS THE LIFE I WAS BORN TO LEAD...
"BUT IT WAS ON A CHILL AUTUMN NIGHT SEVERAL WEEKS LATER, AS AN UNNATURAL MOANING FILTERED THROUGH MY BED CHAMBERS, THAT THE COURSE OF MY LIFE WAS FOREVER SET..."
AAALLFFRREEEDD
EH--?! SOMEONE SOMETHING --CALLING MY NAME! AND MASTER BRUCE AND YOUNG DICK ARE OUT FOR THE EVENING!
PERHAPS IT--IT'S A GHOST!

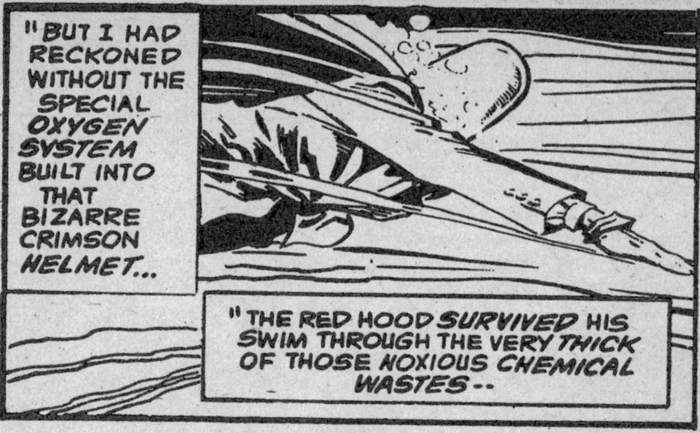
"BUT I HAD RECKONED WITHOUT THE SPECIAL OXYGEN SYSTEM BUILT INTO THAT BIZARRE CRIMSON HELMET...
"THE RED HOOD SURVIVED HIS SWIM THROUGH THE VERY THICK OF THOSE NOXIOUS CHEMICAL WASTES--

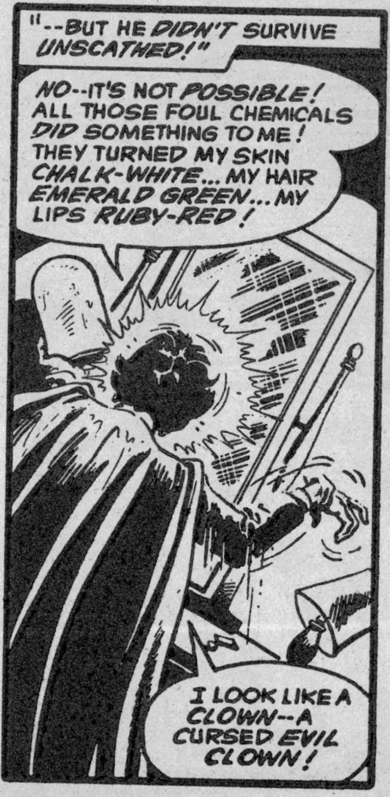
"--BUT HE DIDN'T SURVIVE UNSCATHED!"
NO--IT'S NOT POSSIBLE! ALL THOSE FOUL CHEMICALS DID SOMETHING TO ME! THEY TURNED MY SKIN CHALK-WHITE... MY HAIR EMERALD GREEN... MY LIPS RUBY-RED!
I LOOK LIKE A CLOWN--A CURSED EVIL CLOWN!

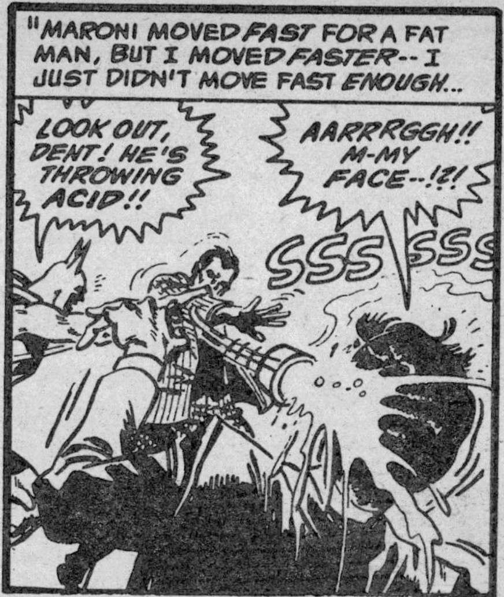
"MARONI MOVED FAST FOR A FAT MAN, BUT I MOVED FASTER-- I JUST DIDN'T MOVE FAST ENOUGH...
LOOK OUT, DENT! HE'S THROWING ACID!!
AARRRGGH!! M-MY FACE--!?!
SSS SSS

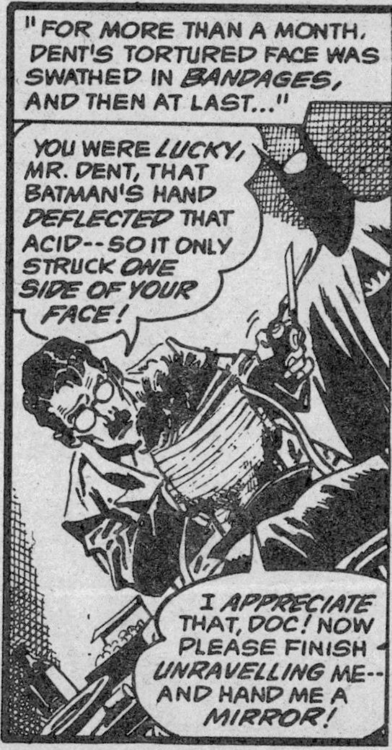
"FOR MORE THAN A MONTH, DENT'S TORTURED FACE WAS SWATHED IN BANDAGES, AND THEN AT LAST..."
YOU WERE LUCKY, MR. DENT, THAT BATMAN'S HAND DEFLECTED THAT ACID--SO IT ONLY STRUCK ONE SIDE OF YOUR FACE!
I APPRECIATE THAT, DOC! NOW PLEASE FINISH UNRAVELLING ME--AND HAND ME A MIRROR!

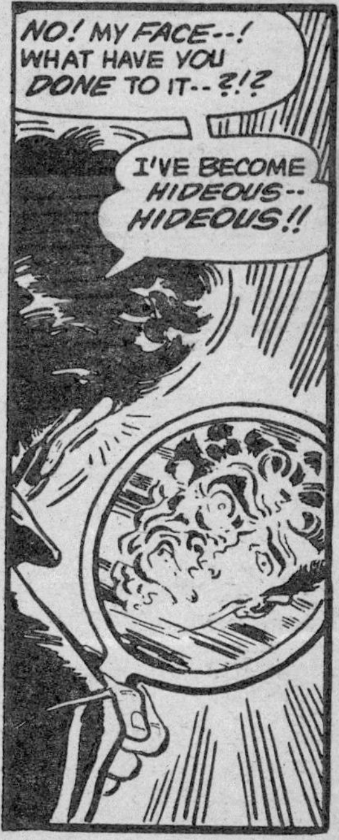
NO! MY FACE--! WHAT HAVE YOU DONE TO IT--?!?
I'VE BECOME HIDEOUS--HIDEOUS!!

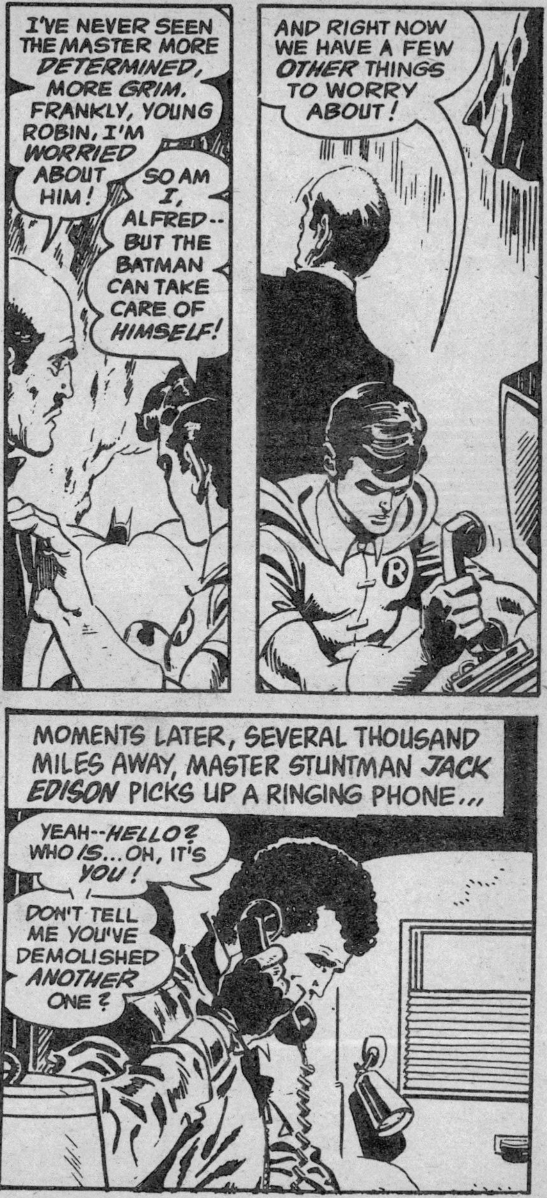
I'VE NEVER SEEN THE MASTER MORE DETERMINED, MORE GRIM. FRANKLY, YOUNG ROBIN, I'M WORRIED ABOUT HIM!
SO AM I, ALFRED-- BUT THE BATMAN CAN TAKE CARE OF HIMSELF!
AND RIGHT NOW WE HAVE A FEW OTHER THINGS TO WORRY ABOUT!
MOMENTS LATER, SEVERAL THOUSAND MILES AWAY, MASTER STUNTMAN JACK EDISON PICKS UP A RINGING PHONE...
YEAH--HELLO? WHO IS...OH, IT'S YOU!
DON'T TELL ME YOU'VE DEMOLISHED ANOTHER ONE?

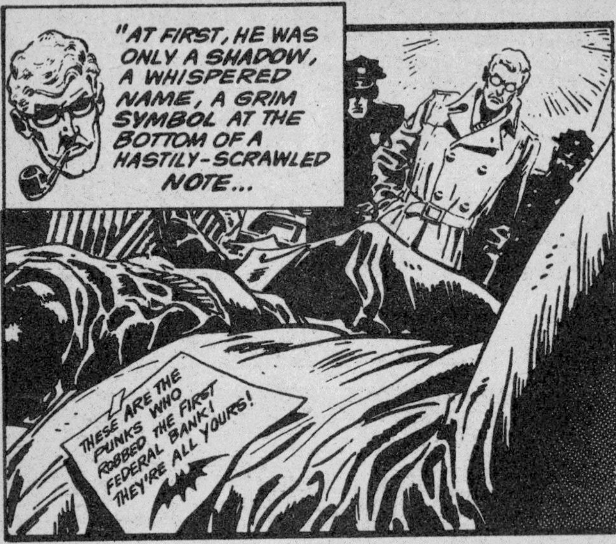
"AT FIRST, HE WAS ONLY A SHADOW, A WHISPERED NAME, A GRIM SYMBOL AT THE BOTTOM OF A HASTILY-SCRAWLED NOTE...
THESE ARE THE PUNKS WHO ROBBED THE FIRST FEDERAL BANK! THEY'RE ALL YOURS!

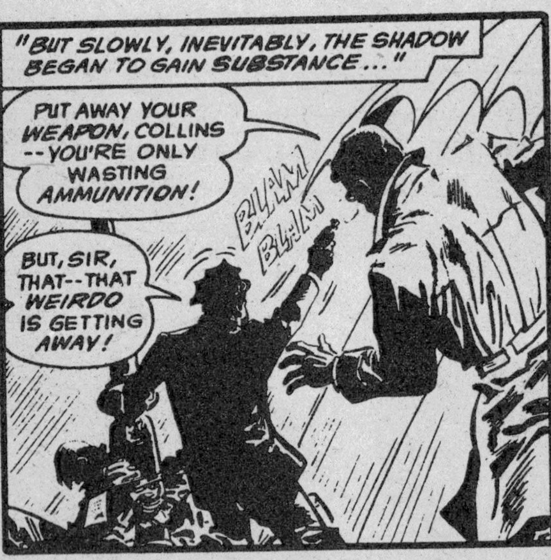
"BUT SLOWLY, INEVITABLY, THE SHADOW BEGAN TO GAIN SUBSTANCE..."
PUT AWAY YOUR WEAPON, COLLINS --YOU'RE ONLY WASTING AMMUNITION!
BLAM
BLAM
BUT, SIR, THAT--THAT WEIRDO IS GETTING AWAY!

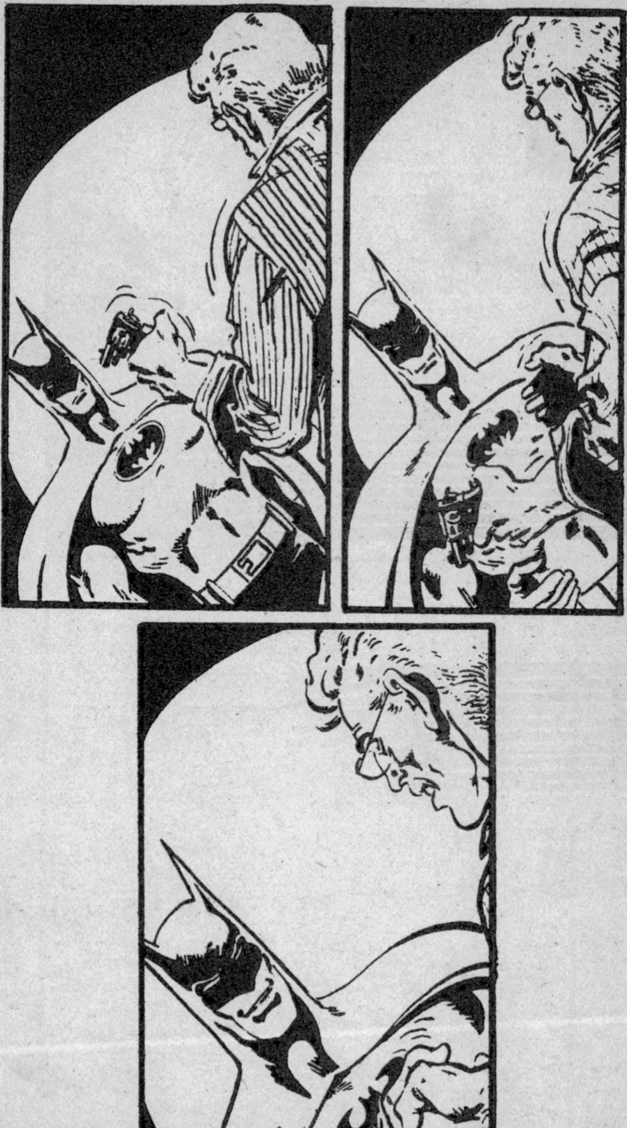

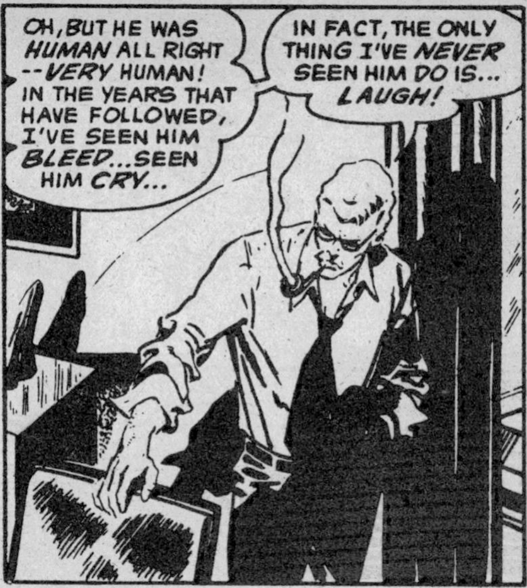
OH, BUT HE WAS HUMAN ALL RIGHT --VERY HUMAN! IN THE YEARS THAT HAVE FOLLOWED, I'VE SEEN HIM BLEED...SEEN HIM CRY...
IN FACT, THE ONLY THING I'VE NEVER SEEN HIM DO IS... LAUGH!

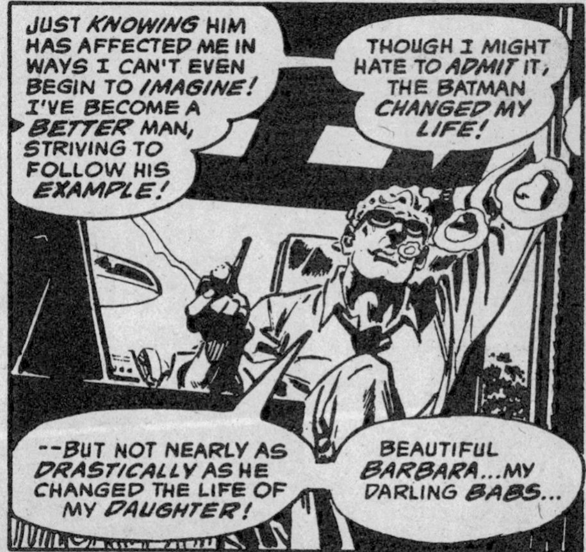
JUST KNOWING HIM HAS AFFECTED ME IN WAYS I CAN'T EVEN BEGIN TO IMAGINE! I'VE BECOME A BETTER MAN, STRIVING TO FOLLOW HIS EXAMPLE!
THOUGH I MIGHT HATE TO ADMIT IT, THE BATMAN CHANGED MY LIFE!
--BUT NOT NEARLY AS DRASTICALLY AS HE CHANGED THE LIFE OF MY DAUGHTER!
BEAUTIFUL BARBARA...MY DARLING BABS...

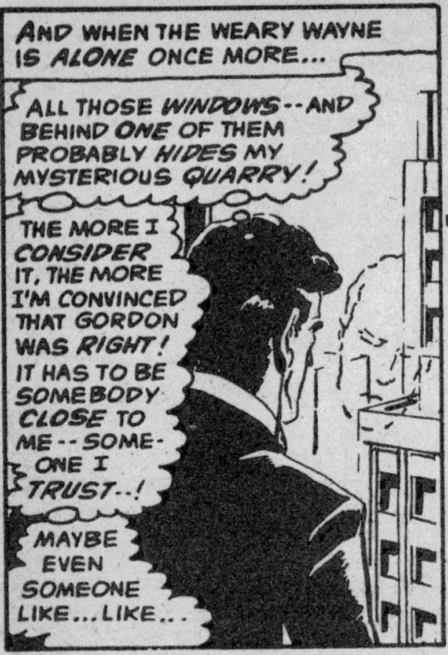
AND WHEN THE WEARY WAYNE IS ALONE ONCE MORE...
ALL THOSE WINDOWS--AND BEHIND ONE OF THEM PROBABLY HIDES MY MYSTERIOUS QUARRY!
THE MORE I CONSIDER IT, THE MORE I'M CONVINCED THAT GORDON WAS RIGHT! IT HAS TO BE SOMEBODY CLOSE TO ME--SOMEONE I TRUST--!
MAYBE EVEN SOMEONE LIKE... LIKE...

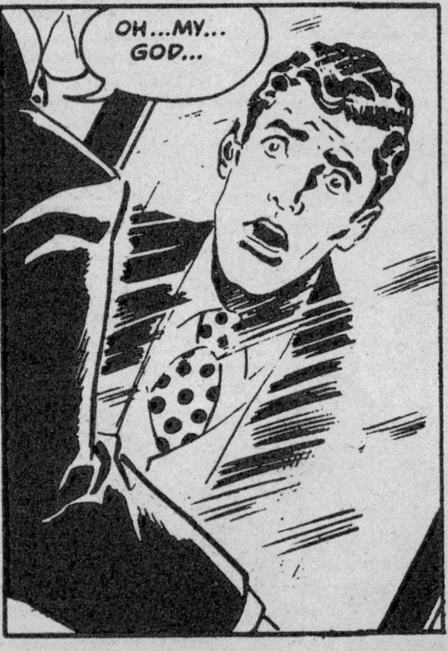
OH...MY... GOD...

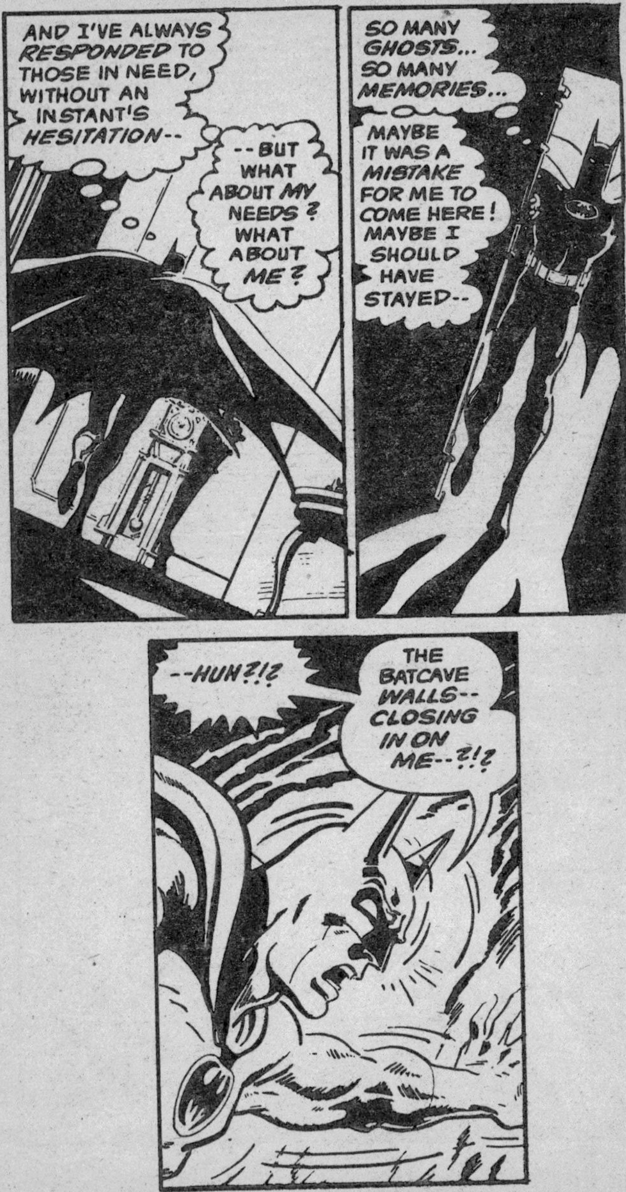
AND I'VE ALWAYS RESPONDED TO THOSE IN NEED, WITHOUT AN INSTANT'S HESITATION--
--BUT WHAT ABOUT MY NEEDS? WHAT ABOUT ME?
SO MANY GHOSTS... SO MANY MEMORIES...
MAYBE IT WAS A MISTAKE FOR ME TO COME HERE! MAYBE I SHOULD HAVE STAYED--
--HUH?!?
THE BATCAVE WALLS--CLOSING IN ON ME--?!?

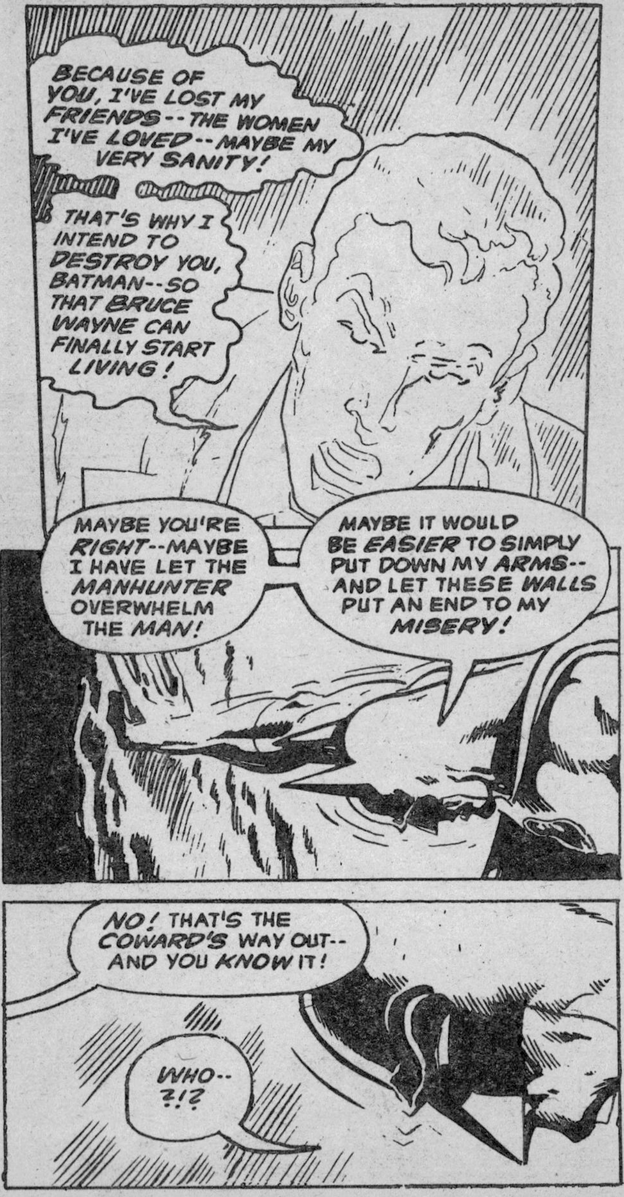

BECAUSE OF YOU, I'VE LOST MY FRIENDS--THE WOMEN I'VE LOVED--MAYBE MY VERY SANITY!
THAT'S WHY I INTEND TO DESTROY YOU, BATMAN--SO THAT BRUCE WAYNE CAN FINALLY START LIVING!
MAYBE YOU'RE RIGHT--MAYBE I HAVE LET THE MANHUNTER OVERWHELM THE MAN!
MAYBE IT WOULD BE EASIER TO SIMPLY PUT DOWN MY ARMS--AND LET THESE WALLS PUT AN END TO MY MISERY!
NO! THAT'S THE COWARD'S WAY OUT--AND YOU KNOW IT!
WHO--?!?

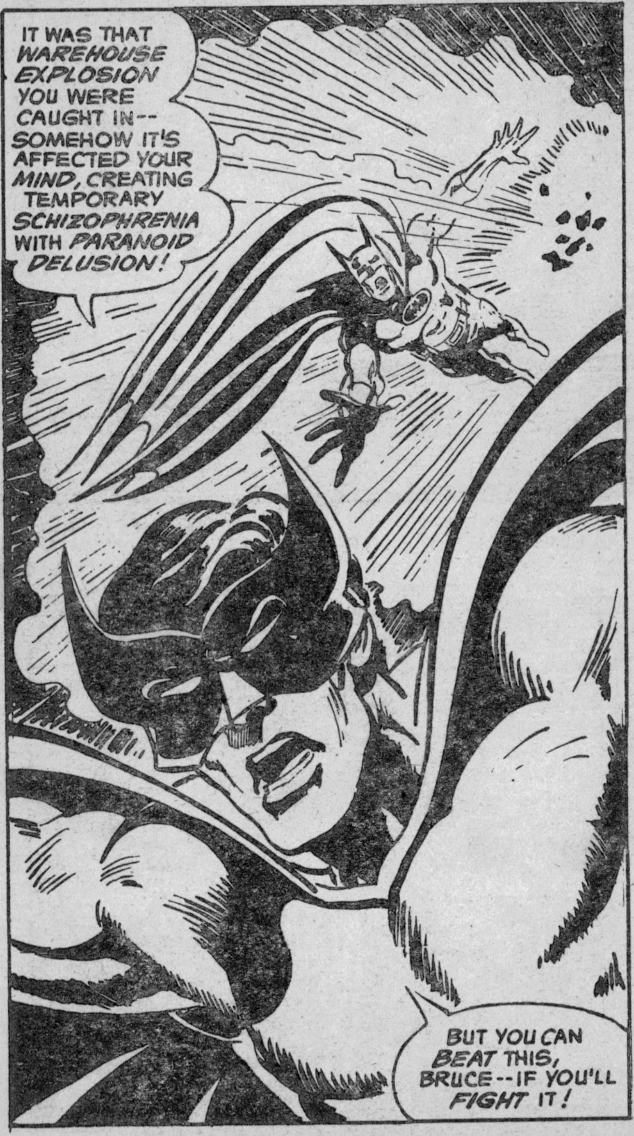
IT WAS THAT WAREHOUSE EXPLOSION YOU WERE CAUGHT IN-- SOMEHOW IT'S AFFECTED YOUR MIND, CREATING TEMPORARY SCHIZOPHRENIA WITH PARANOID DELUSION!
BUT YOU CAN BEAT THIS, BRUCE--IF YOU'LL FIGHT IT!

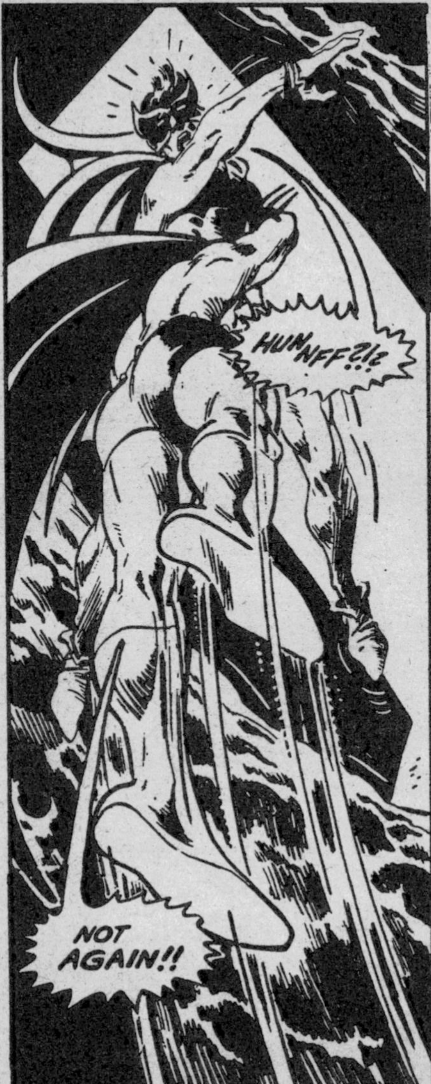
HUNNFF?!?
NOT AGAIN!!

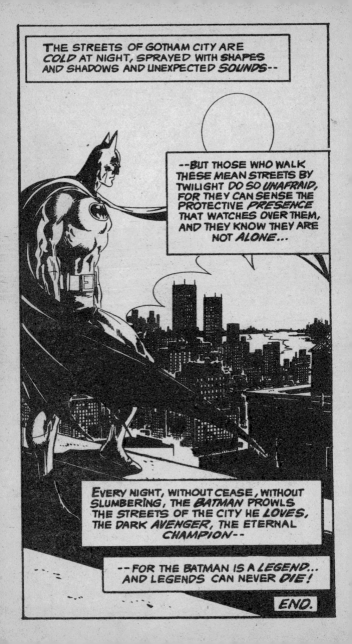